Local perspectives:

foreign aid to the justice sector

This project was funded by The Ford Foundation,
New York and Christian Aid, London

Local perspectives:

foreign aid to the justice sector

Published 2000
International Council on Human Rights Policy
48, chemin du Grand-Montfleury, 1290 Versoix, Switzerland

© Copyright 2000 International Council on Human Rights Policy

Local perspectives: foreign aid to the justice sector
2000, International Council on Human Rights Policy,
Versoix, Switzerland. 132pp.

ISBN 2-940259-04-6

Design and layout by: Aplin Clark, London, UK

Cover illustration © The British Museum. Palestinian Embroidery.
Detail from a head veil, Bethlehem, 19th century.

Printed by: Imprimerie SADAG, Bellegarde/Valserine, France.

CONTENTS

ACKNOWLEDGEMENTS

The Research Team

This report was written by **Craig Mokhiber**, lead researcher for the Council on this project, during a sabbatical from his post with the Office of the United Nations High Commissioner for Human Rights (formerly the UN Centre for Human Rights) where he has worked for several years. Craig Mokhiber is an international human rights lawyer who has extensive experience in the design and implementation of human rights assistance programmes. He has written several human rights manuals and handbooks for the UN and conducted human rights needs assessment, advisory, and training missions for the UN in many countries. From 1996 – 1998 he was Legal Advisor to the UN Special Co-ordinator in the Occupied Territories, where one of his chief tasks involved co-ordinating human rights assistance to the Palestinian National Authority. Prior to joining the United Nations, he worked as an attorney at the New York Bar and as an activist with a number of non-governmental organisations.

Craig Mokhiber was assisted and advised by assistant researchers in the four countries in which field work was conducted:

Bulgaria	Mr **Krassimir Kanev**, Director of the Bulgarian Helsinki Committee.
Cambodia	Mr **Thun Saray**, Director of ADHOC – the Cambodian Human Rights and Development Association.
Guatemala	Mr **Frank La Rue**, founder and Executive Director of CALDH – the Centre for Legal Action on Human Rights.
South Africa	Ms **Corlett Letlojane**, of Africa Affairs Consultancy, who previously worked for several years with Lawyers for Human Rights.

Further assistance was provided by Dessislava Simeonova in Bulgaria, Chun Sath in Cambodia, Jorge Enrique Torres in Guatemala and Motlai Mashilioane and the National Paralegal Institute in South Africa.

We are also grateful to James Sloan, who undertook preliminary consultations on donor programmes in August – September 1998.

The Research Team worked under the supervision of an Advisory Group composed of the following:

Niels Dabelstein, Head of the Evaluation Secretariat, Royal Danish Ministry of Foreign Affairs (DANIDA)

Patricia Feeney, Senior Policy Advisor at OXFAM, (UK)

Marcia Kran, adjunct Professor of Law at the University of British Columbia (Canada) and a consultant with CIDA

Daniel Ravindran, Founder, Asian Forum for Human Rights and Development (Forum-Asia), and a member of the International Council

Justice E.M. Singini, Judge of the High Court of Malawi and Law Commissioner in Malawi

Renate Weber, Co-President, Romanian Helsinki Committee, Director of Open Society Institute in Romania, and a member of the International Council.

A list of people who provided written comments on an earlier draft of this report is provided in Annexe II.

This report was edited by David Petrasek, Research Director at the International Council and the Project Co-ordinator.

PREFACE

Human rights are central to development. Progress cannot be measured in economic terms alone. Moreover, economic progress itself only proceeds in a sustainable way when it is grounded in concern for human rights. In recent years there has been a growing realisation, at all levels, that human rights and development are inextricably linked. Governments, international organisations even financial institutions and business all are, at least in principle, accepting that concern for human rights must guide development efforts.

Yet, if we look at the process of reform in new democracies and countries emerging from dictatorship, it seems that making the commitment to human rights is the easy part. The real challenge is to put that commitment into practice, not least in the administration of justice. New constitutions must be agreed, new laws must be drafted and existing ones reviewed, and judiciaries and police forces reformed and trained. In very poor countries, basic facilities such as courthouses and prisons might be grossly inadequate. Countries emerging from dictatorship and repression cannot easily throw off the legacy of the past. Old institutions have to be reformed, and new institutions created. All of this takes time and resources.

Foreign support for these reform processes is crucial. Outsiders can bring much needed practical and technical advice, as well as the financial resources that are in such short supply. They can help civil society groups get started, bring experience gained elsewhere and alert governments to the steps needed to maintain reform. In many countries, including my own, Malawi, the transition from dictatorship to democracy has relied on support from foreign donors.

Although outside help is needed, the basic responsibility for reforms rests with the national government and domestic institutions. The importance of this point should not be under-estimated. Aid for human rights will fall short of its goal if programmes do not build domestic capacity and ownership. While few would disagree, it is by no means easy in practice to structure programmes in such a way that increases local authority.

For this reason, I am very pleased to introduce this report. It is one of the few efforts to analyse the relatively new flow of aid directed at ensuring that domestic reforms bring greater respect for human rights. Further, its perspective is that of the recipients, those on the receiving end of human rights assistance that is targeted at the justice sector. Building on interviews with beneficiaries, the report provides a number of ideas and suggestions for donors on steps that could be taken to make their programmes more effective. Personally, I feel most privileged to have served on the Advisory Group for the production of this report.

It is my hope that those providing aid, as well as those receiving it, will give due attention to the suggestions made at the end of this report. At the end of the day, if we succeed in ensuring that human rights are better respected, if we can build fair and efficient justice systems, if our police and other institutions act in a way that wins public support for human rights and the rule of law, then all of us will gain.

Justice Elton M. Singini
Law Commissioner, Malawi and
Member of the Malawi Human Rights Commission

INTRODUCTION

As a proportion of overall aid budgets, the amount spent by donor agencies on human rights continues to grow (even as aid budgets are in general decline). Precise statistics for the donor community's expenditure on human rights reform are not available. This is partly because "human rights" was not reported until recently; and partly because countries do not report their expenditure on human rights consistently. One statistic, though certainly too low, comes from the Development Assistance Committee of the OECD, which indicated that in 1998 US$ 241.3m. was committed to aid for "legal and judicial development" and "human rights" by OECD countries (though not all reported). This represented 14% of expenditure reported under "Government and civil society" or about 0.6% of all foreign aid by countries reporting in that year. The figure does not include expenditure in this area by multilateral development banks or UN agencies.[1]

Virtually all donor agencies now integrate human rights concerns into their programmes and policies, though to varying degrees. The programmes concerned are not necessarily called "human rights assistance" – relevant transfers fall within aid for "governance", for "democratic reform", and support for "the rule of law" – and no consistent reporting system has been set up so that it remains difficult to separate funding for human rights from other categories of aid. The fact remains, nonetheless, that this component of international assistance is increasingly important, and is having increasingly visible effects on institutions in many countries.

What impact is this assistance having? How could it be made more effective? What types of programmes are achieving results? To what extent does this type of assistance differ from development assistance in general? What specific problems arise in providing this type of aid? Which types of donor agencies (bilateral, multilateral, private) are best equipped to provide it?

In August 1998, the International Council on Human Rights Policy began research into some of these questions, with the objective of understanding what forms of human rights assistance are effective. After initial consultation, we decided to focus on beneficiaries of human rights programmes – the government departments, judicial institutions and non-governmental organisations that receive the assistance. What do they believe are the problems? How do they think aid for human rights reform could be improved? We prioritised the views of local organisations because human rights reform cannot be sustained without their commitment and participation; in the end, therefore, they determine the success of aid. To make the research manageable, we chose four countries – Bulgaria, Cambodia, Guatemala and South Africa – and concentrated on programmes that provide assistance to the administration of justice.

---

[1] We provide a brief overview of the main agencies and their policies on human rights assistance in Annexe III.

This study sets out the results of our research and presents the views of the beneficiaries we interviewed. Their view, overwhelmingly, is that human rights aid has been an essential ingredient in advancing respect for human rights. At the same time, many donor programmes fall short of their objectives. Beneficiaries identified several reasons for failure – confusion about how human rights relates to broader development efforts; political factors and fears that hinder the provision of aid where and when it is most needed; lack of planning and failure to adopt a strategic approach; insufficient attention to local context and needs. Above all, perhaps, beneficiaries felt that their views and experience are given too little weight. They fear that aid for human rights reform, so important for their countries, will repeat the mistakes made in development assistance more generally.

The report is divided into 7 chapters. After a short section on terms and methodology, in chapter 2 we survey some of the key political and social issues in the countries we visited. Chapters 3, 4, 5 and 6 deal in turn with four key areas, basing the analysis throughout on the 150 interviews the research team conducted with beneficiary and donor organisations.

- What is the relationship between human rights and development?
- What problems are particular to human rights assistance?
- The need for more strategic approaches to reform.
- Improving relations between donors and beneficiaries.

Chapter 7 sets out our conclusions and findings.

We should begin with one caveat, and one plea. The literature on development is complex and extensive. Even within the narrower category of aid for human rights reform, there is much expertise in donor agencies, beneficiary institutions and research institutions. We could not hope, and did not intend, to cover all the relevant issues. Our purpose was in fact quite limited – to describe the concerns of those who receive aid. One piece of a broader picture.

This study is not intended to be a definitive account of foreign aid for human rights reform. It surveys the views of one set of actors involved in the aid process – and, even then, picks from a small group of countries. This said, we believe that those we interviewed made points that should be heard by donors as well as recipients of aid. Though the report provides few answers and many of the questions it raises are undoubtedly difficult to resolve, it plants signposts and suggests some directions. We hope it may be a useful map that people on both sides of the aid exchange can use to make progress in the long dialogue that inevitably unites and divides them. Might it be a point of departure for deeper discussion of hard issues in an area of work that is of fundamental importance for the long-term protection of human rights? That would be our plea.

One: **METHODOLOGY AND DEFINITION OF TERMS**

Methodology

This chapter briefly explains the focus of our research, how the research was done, and the way we use certain terms in this report. It concludes by explaining why we chose to prioritise the views of beneficiaries.

Human rights assistance offers a potentially vast field of enquiry – and a still large one after we had focused our research on the perspective of beneficiaries. To make the research manageable we therefore selected four focus countries for research, and limited ourselves to assistance programmes dealing with the administration of justice.

The four countries chosen for study were Bulgaria, Cambodia, Guatemala and South Africa. These countries were selected for several reasons, including the nature of their reform process, the scale and number of human rights assistance programmes, and regional diversity. Chapter 3 provides a snapshot of the reform process in each of these countries.

We chose to focus on the administration of justice because it is the target of much human rights assistance. The justice sector provides not only a rich sample for study, but impacts directly on all human rights – civil and political, as well as economic, social and cultural (although of course, in many countries it pays insufficient attention to the latter category). In addition, the justice sector is central to a rights-based approach to development, because it includes the bodies that must enforce and give effect to those rights.

While we have focused on this one area, we hope the study and its findings throw some light on the strengths and weaknesses of human rights assistance more generally. Some, at least, of the comments we report, and the findings, apply to human rights and development assistance as a whole.

The lead researcher conducted interviews in the focus countries. In each country he was accompanied and advised by a national research consultant. Those interviewed included beneficiaries in government, public institutions, and civil society, and other relevant actors in the country (such as academics or staff in research institutions). In addition, in each of the countries we interviewed staff representing aid organisations of all kinds. In all, more than 150 interviews were conducted in the four countries from May to October 1999.

Separate from interviews in the four countries, we also met with staff in donor agencies. Prior to identifying the research focus for the project, such staff were consulted in Brussels, Geneva, London, New York, Ottawa and Paris (in bilateral development agencies, international development banks and United Nations (UN) agencies). At the beginning of the research process, further interviews were held with donor agencies in Brussels, Geneva, Ottawa and Washington.

In early January 2000, the Council sent out a draft of this report for consultation. Over 350 individuals were approached, including those who had been interviewed in the course of the research, staff in donor agencies, beneficiaries in other countries receiving human rights assistance, and relevant academic and research institutions. The draft report did not include explicit findings or recommendations, but set out the main results of the research. We received over 40 substantive comments from those who received the draft report. The present report, which was finalised in March and April 2000, takes those comments into account.

While we refer to some written sources, the analysis is based primarily on interviews. A select bibliography of literature consulted in the course of the research is provided in the Bibliography.

Our understanding of local context draws on the advice of nationals in each of the focus countries, including those we interviewed and in particular the local research consultants who worked closely with the lead researcher in each of the countries. In some cases, donors and foreign specialists and academics may take different views. They may differ on interpretations of fact and their reading of the history of development efforts in a given country. Our first aim has been to reflect and analyse the perspectives of national beneficiaries, as faithfully as we could, given the particular focus of this study.

The study adopts an approach of not attributing comments. There is a need for a frank and critical exchange on beneficiary experiences, and we feel some responsibility to avoid complicating or even jeopardising assistance relationships. In addition, we accepted advice from donors and beneficiaries who felt attribution would be unhelpful. Thus, by design, and by agreement with those interviewed, comments are generally not attributed (unless such comments were received in writing).

This study is not an evaluation of particular donor programmes or projects. Many evaluations are conducted each year by or on behalf of the donors mentioned in this report, and readers interested in programme evaluations should consult the sources cited in Annex III. This study also does not provide a detailed survey of the human rights situation in any country.

Definition of terms

Language and terminology are important factors in any field of study. The use of particular terms in the development and human rights fields elicits strong reactions from practitioners and academics. The term "beneficiary" leads to debate about who actually benefits most from aid. The term "donor" is disliked by some providers of assistance, who do not consider themselves to be simple funders but to be working in solidarity with national NGOs. Some think "assistance" is an outdated and patronising term, and prefer to use "co-operation". Since there exists no universally agreed glossary of standardised terminology in these fields, organisations use different terms to refer to the same things. Solely to facilitate our discussion, we provide here our working definitions of key terms used in this report.

Human rights assistance

We use the term *human rights assistance* to name the type of activity that is the subject of this study. It is not used universally by donors. As noted above, many donors prefer the word "co-operation" to assistance, thereby emphasising the quality of the relationship between donor and beneficiary – the partnership it is meant to involve. Some important donors (in terms of resources applied and number of programmes) deny that they provide aid to human rights as such. The World Bank, for example, generally considers that its Articles do not permit the Bank to provide aid that focuses on human rights. The Bank therefore uses terms like support for *legal development* or *judicial reform* to refer to programmes that are relevant to this study. Both the Bank and the United Nations Development Programme (UNDP) often speak of *governance* when they refer to programmes which deal (at least in part) with what others would call human rights assistance. Other donors have programmes that promote *democratisation* or the *rule of law*, while the United Nations (UN) refers to *advisory services in the field of human rights*. The list of terms is long and is used flexibly by different aid providers.

By human rights assistance we mean, simply, *development aid expressly targeted to strengthen institutions an reform processes with the aim of improving domestic capacity to promote and protect human rights*.[2] It can be argued that all development aid is human rights assistance, since it is given to improve health, education, housing, and other subjects of human rights norms. Some reject this approach, however. They point to the legal nature of rights and insist that, to qualify as human rights assistance, activities must focus on establishing or improving legal guarantees (to health, to education, to freedom from torture, etc.). Many donors have traditionally been even more restrictive. In most cases they have equated human rights assistance with programmes that support the rule of law, the administration of justice, national human rights commissions, or human rights NGOs.

In our view, the former approach is too broad, and the latter two are too restrictive. For our purpose, the key is the *stated objective* of a given programme. To the extent that its objectives expressly relate to building the capacity of institutions that advance or protect human rights, a programme may be said to qualify as human rights assistance. Under this definition, the term includes technical co-operation projects related to health, education, housing, justice administration, elections, labour and personal security. For purposes of this study,

---

[2] The term "institution building" in this definition is not intended to exclude any area of relevant assistance, and would thus include interventions targeting legislation, awareness raising, training and so on. There is, however, an implicit presumption that donors support or build local capacity to do those things, rather than do them directly.

it does not include humanitarian assistance, or general human rights promotional activities (i.e., not directed to building institutional capacity).

Justice sector

In this study *justice sector* refers to all national institutions, laws and policies established to administer both criminal and civil justice, including legal regulation and monitoring. This definition covers institutions in all three branches of government (executive, legislature and judicial), as well as independent national institutions such as human rights commissions and ombudsman offices. In particular, we refer to courts, prosecutors, legal education institutions, parliaments, police, prison administrations, ministries of justice and the interior (or their equivalents), and related institutions.

In addition, we include in our definition of the justice sector non-governmental organisations that are directly involved in the administration of justice, either as parts of the system or as independent monitors of its legality, fairness and effectiveness. Examples might be human rights NGOs working on justice issues, associations of defence lawyers or legal aid lawyers or bar associations, and organisations offering paralegal support.

As we use it, therefore, the term has a more narrow designation than the *rule of law* sector as defined by the UN (which includes, for example, the mass media, electoral authorities and the military). At the same time it has a broader application than the term *judicial reform* used by some bilateral donors to refer exclusively to aid that is given to courts and ministries of justice. In general, our starting point is that justice should be considered as a *sector*, in the same way that development agencies consider that education and health and the environment are distinct sectors. Such sectors are not simple objects and certainly cannot be detached from their wider social and political contexts; but they help donors and beneficiaries to recognise that sustainable progress requires a strategic approach that will strengthen and relate the work of many kinds of institutions. Chapter 4 explains in more detail the implications of seeing justice as a sector and including relevant non-governmental organisations within it.

Types of assistance

We have included all forms of human rights assistance directed at the justice sector, including *grants, loans, advisory services, technical assistance, training, publication support, fellowships and scholarships, equipment provision, infrastructure development, planning and co-ordination support*, and others, whether they support national law or policy-making functions, justice administration, law enforcement, monitoring and casework, education, or any other function within the justice sector.

Actors and roles: donors and beneficiaries

The delivery of aid, including human rights assistance to the justice sector, is rarely a bilateral affair between donor and recipient. It is typically a chain, involving multiple links in the donor country, and more in the recipient country. Official bilateral donors like Sweden's SIDA or Australia's AUSAID, and multilateral donors like the European Commission, sometimes provide assistance directly to recipient organisations in the targeted country. But they might also channel their aid through independent organisations based in donor countries or through international organisations like the United Nations. The assistance provided may be in the form of funding, advice, or a combination of both. Non-profit, private and non-governmental organisations also act as channels for official aid. When they do, they may be considered to be both beneficiaries and donors, since they pass on part of the resources they receive to institutions in a recipient country.

The chain of actors may include a primary donor (such as USAID), a donor-country implementing agency (an NGO based in the donor country), a beneficiary-country partner (a national NGO in the recipient country), a primary beneficiary (a police training academy), secondary beneficiaries (police recruits), and ultimate beneficiaries (the citizens of a given police district, or detainees as a class). If an official donor provides ten thousand dollars to an NGO in its own country, and this NGO provides a training course to an audience in a developing country, it may be asked: who is the donor and who the beneficiary? Needless to say, these are complex relationships, and not captured easily by simple terms such as "donor" and "beneficiary".

To distinguish donors and beneficiaries in this study, we look first and foremost at the boundary between foreign and domestic – the point where external resources are turned over to internal groups and institutions, and where domestic justice sector institutions and actors come face to face with foreign institutions and actors. To focus our analysis and simplify discussion, we call one side of this exchange the donor (or provider), and the other side the beneficiary (or recipient). Actors on both sides of the exchange sometimes adopt and sometimes reject this terminology, and we make no judgement as to its general validity. We have adopted these terms primarily for ease of reference and, where it is possible or more appropriate, we have used language that is more precise.

Beneficiaries (recipients)

We use the terms *beneficiaries* and *recipients* to refer to national recipients of human rights assistance, while recognising that "benefit" can be derived by a donor, a beneficiary, or a third party (such as a donor country contractor), by any combination of the three, or by no one at all. Beneficiaries exist at many levels in the justice sector (as elsewhere). In any final analysis, of course, the "beneficiaries" are not national institutions in the justice sector (or those who staff them), but those people who stand to benefit from a better justice system. This would include criminal defendants, prisoners, members of minority communities, victims of crime and abuse of power, and indeed the general population. For this study, however, we use the term "beneficiaries" for the most part to refer to those institutions and organisations in the recipient country who receive foreign assistance. In doing so, we recognise the need for further research to be done into the positions, opinions and perspectives of the broader public (the true "beneficiaries") and, in particular, those most exposed to abuse or discrimination, in the justice system as elsewhere. These groups include, among others, prisoners, women, the poor and minorities.

Donors (providers)

We use *donor* (or provider) to refer to all external providers of any form of aid (loans, grants, technical assistance). We include bilateral and multilateral donors in the strict sense (such as Danida, SIDA, USAID, the European Union – EU); international agencies (notably UN programmes); international and regional financial institutions (such as the World Bank or the Asian Development Bank); and international NGOs, consultancy firms and private foundations.

Donors play a variety of roles in the reform and development context. A typology of assistance might distinguish projects

- funded and implemented by donors; funded by donors and implemented by foreign organisations; or funded by donors and implemented by local organisations;
- designed by donors; designed by foreign organisations; or designed by local organisations;
- where the donor is an NGO, the implementer is an NGO and the beneficiary is an NGO; where the donor, the implementer and the beneficiary are government agencies; or any combination of the above; and
- that involve funding; that involve advice; that involve a combination of both.

Further divisions could be made. While recognising the diversity of actors and interests, we still feel the term "donor" best captures the essential function involved.

Government and non-government

A number of those who commented on an earlier version of this study questioned the wisdom of lumping both official government institutions and independent non-governmental organisations together on both sides of the aid equation. Does it make sense to call both the judiciary and a legal watch-dog NGO "beneficiaries", especially when the latter spends much time criticising the arbitrariness of the former? Likewise, is it helpful to call both official bilateral aid agencies and private foundations "donors" – especially when the latter feel they have more in common with the NGO partners they assist?

As noted above, we chose to draw the line between external providers and domestic recipients, but recognise that other divisions are possible. However, it was interesting that on many issues we found little disagreement between government and non-government beneficiaries. It might well be that beneficiaries share more than had been realised in their experiences, and that opinions vary more on the donor side between official and non-governmental providers.

The beneficiary perspective

An approach that prioritises beneficiary perspectives (over those of donors) may be seen to have certain risks, both methodologically and politically. We explain here why we think, despite these risks, such an approach is both useful and justified.

No externally conceived and imposed programme of assistance could ever hope to take root, effect meaningful change, or remain sustainable after the departure of the aid provider. For this reason alone, it is essential to take due account of – indeed direction from – the perspective of the beneficiaries. To do so is a point of principle but also is an important practical requirement for successful human rights assistance. This is the central reason for putting the beneficiary perspective near the heart of any analysis of such programmes.

Other arguments for doing so can also be made. Beneficiaries have few means of advancing their concerns in international debates about aid for human rights reforms. Beneficiaries themselves are acutely aware, and often highly critical of the power imbalance that lies behind the development "partnership". Most argue that "paying the fiddler" still means "calling the tune", so that the aid provided often responds more directly to the wants of the donor than to the needs of the domestic constituencies to be (at least nominally) served. Beneficiaries do not usually have their own co-ordination committees, nationally or internationally, to act as a unified counterpart to donor co-ordination structures at both levels. The Development Assistance Committee (DAC) of the Organisation for Economic Co-operation and Development (OECD), for example, brings together official donors at the international level to co-ordinate development policies. Donors also meet in World Bank co-ordinated consultative group meetings, United Nations Development Programme (UNDP) roundtables, and so on. Beneficiaries have no such cross-border institutions, and rarely even benefit from a national version. They may have government committees and NGO coalitions, but almost never a body that unites the two sides. In this unbalanced context, it is helpful to enable beneficiaries from several countries, and from both sides of the government/NGO divide, to voice their concerns.

Donors consult with beneficiaries, of course, and, at official level, memoranda and agreements are signed that take account of the views and needs of institutions receiving assistance. Donor agencies also conduct regular evaluations of their projects and these should, in theory, include the views of beneficiaries. Even so, beneficiaries told us that they have rarely been consulted at length on these matters. While many donors have conducted programme reviews and evaluations in recent years – some of which contain frank, objective and critical analysis and some of which draw on the views of beneficiaries – on the whole such reviews are conducted by or on behalf of providers, and thus focus on the provider's perspective. We see it as worthwhile, in this context, to draw out the points of view of beneficiaries in more detail.

Where donors themselves evaluate assistance programmes, it is always difficult to know whether beneficiaries will answer frankly and critically. In many cases, future programmes and employment are at risk. Beneficiaries will not hurry to "bite the hand that feeds them". They are more likely to comment frankly when an independent organisation, unconnected to the programmes concerned, asks the same questions. In this project, we have interviewed beneficiaries on the express understanding that they will not be quoted by name or organisation (unless they otherwise agree). The result, we believe, has been a wealth of critical (and thus useful) commentary.

In prioritising the views of beneficiaries we do not assume however, that their views are necessarily correct in all cases. Some argue that, since beneficiaries have an interest in the aid concerned, their opinions are not impartial and should be discounted to some degree. Some will also say that in many cases beneficiaries are in receipt of aid because the institutions or organisations for which they work are not self-sustaining and may be ineffective. With regard to training and advice, knowledge – about international standards, and effective institutions – is precisely the "product" which they have appealed to assistance providers to deliver.

However, if beneficiaries have an "interest", this is not a reason to discount their views. Donors too have interests – official assistance for human rights is rarely immune from foreign policy considerations. Donor views are not necessarily more objective or impartial. In fact, the direct "interest" which beneficiaries have in the scope and content of reform is itself a good reason to give attention to their views. Similarly, one should not dismiss domestic competence and assume foreign wisdom. High levels of practical expertise exist in all societies, organisations and contexts, regardless of poverty or other factors. Our exchanges with beneficiaries have revealed rich domestic sources of expertise, creativity and competence in all of the countries involved. They have also revealed some cases of remarkably unskilled foreign advisors and agencies. While the international and comparative expertise of foreign advisors is to be valued, experience in numerous countries shows that local understanding of context and culture and political tradition is vital to the design of successful development and aid programmes. Without access to such essentially *domestic* knowledge, international expertise, however sophisticated, will lead to errors. It is this understanding that underpins the ideas of partnership and participation.

Finally, we should say that in prioritising the views of beneficiaries in this study, we are guided by the notion that individuals have a right to participate actively in the development process – a right recognised in the UN Declaration on the Right to Development. Giving due weight, therefore, to local perspectives is not just a practical necessity for effective aid programmes. The primacy of the perspective of domestic actors on how justice sector reform should be conceived and managed is itself required by the notions of participation and self-determination that are central to the right to development and indeed lie at the core of human rights.

Two: **THE NATIONAL REFORM CONTEXT –**
BULGARIA, CAMBODIA, GUATEMALA AND SOUTH AFRICA

Bulgaria, Cambodia, Guatemala and South Africa are all countries in which dramatic transition processes occurred in the 1990s. In all four, too, human rights assistance has been a central factor in (unfinished) efforts to institutionalise reforms. Our consultations in those countries revealed many interesting lessons for human rights assistance. One was that development processes, and therefore programmes to establish human rights, cannot be well understood if they are analysed only at the national level.[3] There are important distinctions between the developed and largely white South Africa and its poor and black majority; between the Guatemala of the "white Ladinos" of the capital and that of the poor, rural and Mayan majority; between the Bulgaria of the national majority, and that of the poorer, less empowered Roma and Muslim minorities; and between the Cambodia of the Khmer man of Phnom Penh, and that of the ethnic Vietnamese woman in the rural provinces.

At the same time, interesting comparisons can be made between justice reform efforts in these countries. At the beginning of the 1990s, Cambodia and Guatemala were locked in bloody civil wars, Bulgaria was subject to authoritarian repression and South Africa was still under *apartheid* rule. Racism in all four countries, both official and popular, indicated their failure to broadly secure human dignity. Turks and Moslems in Bulgaria, ethnic Vietnamese in Cambodia, indigenous Mayans in Guatemala and black South Africans all suffered severe discrimination. Official ideologies of repression and discrimination (including virulent forms of nationalism, "state security" doctrines and institutionalised racism) remained in place even if their force was weakening. Yet the political environments in all four countries were transformed with extraordinary rapidity. Today, Bulgaria has a democratically elected government, Cambodia's war has ended, Guatemala is implementing peace accords based on human rights guarantees, and South Africa has elected its second President on the basis of universal franchise.

While these achievements are not necessarily secure, there is no doubt that all four countries have been transformed in the last ten years, probably irreversibly. While human rights assistance programmes were not a determining factor in launching these reforms, in every case they became important to carrying them forward. By way of introduction, we set out below a brief profile of each country.

---

[3] Or, for that matter, by region. Commentators have rightly pointed out, for example, that South Africa's experience differs significantly from that of other nations in sub-Saharan Africa. (*Communication to the Council from DFID officials*, March 2000).

Bulgaria

When the Berlin Wall fell a decade ago, it shook the foundations beneath the authoritarian order that had ruled Bulgaria for four decades. However, though Bulgaria's transition began in 1989, reform started slowly. A new democratic constitution was adopted in 1991. *De jure*, if not yet *de facto*, it introduced a legal and political order marked by clear separation of powers, multi-party democracy, an independent judiciary, and an elected and accountable legislature and executive. From 1991 to 1997, reform was paralysed by numerous changes of government, mismanagement, political conflict and severe economic decline. This period ended when massive public protests led to the election in 1997 of a reform minded government – the beginning, say Bulgarians, of real reforms in the country.

At least in economic and social terms, for many Bulgarians the post-communist decade has brought decline rather than progress. Bulgaria remains one of the poorest countries in the region. A third of its people live in poverty. The situation of Roma communities is much worse. Four out of five live below the poverty line. Infant mortality rates have risen, maternal mortality is among the highest in Europe, and life expectancy, low for the region, actually declined during the 1990s. The quality of basic education has fallen, enrolment rates are down, and drop-out rates have risen.

The new legal system lacks technical, physical and human resources. It is trusted by very few. There is low public confidence in the police. Crime rates are high and the police do not have adequate resources to deal with the demands made on them. Prisons are neglected, dilapidated, under-resourced, and largely unreformed. However, the basic legal framework is established. Constitutionally, the judicial branch is independent – including the courts, prosecutors, and investigating bodies charged with preliminary criminal investigation. The court system includes the Constitutional Court, the Supreme Court of Cassation, the Supreme Administrative Court, courts of appeal, of assizes and district courts. A Supreme Judicial Council is the country's judicial oversight body, responsible for the election, promotion, assignment and disciplining of judges, prosecutors and investigating magistrates.[4]

Unquestionably, the most powerful single force driving reform is the current government's eagerness to achieve EU membership. The push to accession touches upon government (and donor) action in every sector, including justice. NGOs have harnessed this force to make strategic human rights gains, by accessing the European Court, lobbying European donors, and citing European standards in their efforts to enhance local democracy, increase government accountability, and defend vulnerable groups. Beyond this, beneficiaries on both sides of the government/NGO divide affirmed that human rights assistance has

---

[4] *De jure*, although, observers say, it lacks the capacity to do so *de facto*.

itself had an important impact, contributing to the development of sophisticated human rights organisations throughout the decade and, most recently, helping to build the framework for broad justice sector reform and development.

Cambodia

Cambodian history in the past century is a tragic one. Colonised by France, bombed by the United States, decimated by the Khmer Rouge, and then torn apart by civil war, Cambodia's reconstruction did not begin until October 1991, when the Paris Peace Agreements were signed. Almost six years after the last UN peacekeeping forces left, Cambodia is only now emerging from a state of extended emergency and beginning to develop its institutions. Any fair assessment of Cambodia's progress in recent years must take account of this background, before considering how far there is to go.

Today, Cambodia is still a very poor country.[5] Almost 40 percent of Cambodians live below the poverty line. Half Cambodia's children under five years of age suffer from malnutrition. School enrolment rates are low and drop-out rates are high. The rate of infant mortality is the highest in the sub-region, and the rate of HIV/AIDS infection is one of the highest in Asia. Malaria, tuberculosis and acute respiratory infections are leading causes of morbidity. Land mines laid during the war continue to maim and kill and stifle rural development.

Cambodia's hybrid legal system is also deeply influenced by the country's history. It is built mostly on French civil law, to which have been added elements of socialist approaches (de facto) and common law systems (acquired since 1992).[6] Especially in rural areas, some indigenous conflict resolution traditions survive, alongside the official legal system largely developed in the French colonial period (1863 to independence in 1953). That system was erased by the Khmer Rouge when "Democratic Kampuchea" was established in 1975. All national laws and institutions were abolished and most of the country's lawyers, judges, justice officials, and intellectuals were murdered, starved to death or fled (together with millions of their compatriots). When the Khmer Rouge were driven from power by Vietnamese forces in 1979, genocide was followed by civil war, which continued until the Peace Accords were signed in Paris in 1991. A socialist legal tradition was in force from 1981 to 1991. From 1991 an entirely new legal order was established, which resurrected in amended form the original civil law tradition. A series of "transitional" laws were adopted in 1992 and 1993 when, under the Peace Accords, the United Nations Transitional Authority in Cambodia (UNTAC)

---

[5] According to the 1999 UNDP *Human Development Report*, Cambodia ranks 137 out of 174 countries.

[6] Most of the common law influence is also *de facto*, resulting from the concentration of common law foreign legal advisers working in the country in the 1990's. Some common law principles are making their way into developing commercial legislation, but public law remains dominated by the French civil law tradition. (Koy Neam, Asia Foundation office in Cambodia, *Communication to the Council*, March 2000).

took on numerous government functions until elections were held and a new constitution was promulgated. Many of the so-called "UNTAC laws" continue in force today.

Though these efforts are far from complete, and many problems remain, remarkable progress has been made. When we asked beneficiaries whether human rights assistance has had a positive impact in Cambodia, they all agreed it had. One leading Khmer human rights activist called the impact of human rights assistance "enormous", adding that "without the important support of the donors since 1991, Cambodia would have no NGOs, no democratic constitution, no free press, and no hope".

Guatemala

When local human rights activists talked to us about reforms, they often reflected on the horror of Guatemala's civil war. When asked to describe improvements, they did not speak of more courts, better police or enhanced access to lawyers, but of fewer massacres, summary executions, and disappearances – all constant features of the previous decades. The Commission for Historical Clarification (the truth commission established under the peace accords) has estimated that more than 200,000 Guatemalans were killed or disappeared in 30 years of civil war, a period in which the justice system was itself part of the mechanism of repression. According to the Commission, the judicial authorities tolerated and even facilitated the violence, and sheltered repressive officials.

Today, Guatemala remains a deeply unequal society. In terms of wealth and power, in urban as well as rural areas, the indigenous majority are sharply disadvantaged. Guatemala has one of the world's widest income inequalities and land distribution is dramatically unbalanced. Especially among indigenous people, schooling levels and literacy rates are low. Over one-third of Guatemalan men and over half the country's women are illiterate. Extreme poverty is widespread among rural indigenous communities.

The Guatemalan legal system is framed by the Constitution and the Civil Code and built on a civil law model. Police and prisons are administered by a *Ministerio de Gobernacíon*. Investigations and prosecutions are conducted by a *Ministerio Publico*. State legal counsel is provided by an Attorney General (*Procuradoria General de la Nacíon*). The judicial branch is composed of a Supreme Court (which is both the highest court and the administrator of the judiciary), courts of appeal, courts of first instance, and justices of the peace. The country also has a constitutional court and a human rights ombudsman (*Procuradoria de Derechos Humanos*). An Institute of Public Defence (*Instituto de Servicio Publico de Defensa Penal*) has also been established. A parallel system of traditional indigenous law and conflict resolution functions in Mayan communities.[7]

Assessing progress in the Guatemalan justice sector depends on the period of comparison. As a Guatemalan jurist pointed out to us, the first (foreign-supported) justice-reform process took place in 1836 when the Livingston Codes, drawn up by a US jurist from Louisiana, were introduced. This experiment, which lasted two years until the overthrow of the government, was the first of many failed initiatives. In the 1980s, donor-supported projects, ostensibly to strengthen the rule of law, ended in failure because political authorities were not committed to reform. Real opportunity for meaningful reform did not emerge until Guatemala's civil war ended and comprehensive peace accords were signed, built largely on human rights guarantees and international verification. By most accounts, therefore, 1997 is the starting point for the reform process. Today, many donors support programmes to reform the justice system in the courts, prosecution and police services among others. While it is too early to talk about impact, this commitment of resources (over US$80 million by some estimates) is being welcomed by both human rights NGOs and official institutions in the country.

South Africa

More than three centuries of colonialism and more than fifty years of *apartheid* have left their mark on every aspect of South African life. Multi-racial elections and the dismantling of *apartheid* laws and institutions have not erased these traces, which show themselves in deeply entrenched inequality, poverty and violence. For reformers in the justice sector, struggling at once with the challenge of transformation and with high levels of crime, violence and a multitude of new demands from previously excluded communities, *apartheid*'s legacy seems omnipresent.

While post-*apartheid* South Africa emerges as a single, unified and multi-racial state, in economic and social terms it is still two countries in one.[8] World Bank statistics point to a dual reality in which white South Africa ranks in 18th place globally (in economic terms), on a par with New Zealand, while black South Africa stands 118th, close to Lesotho and Vietnam. Fewer than 50 per cent of black South Africans have a primary school education, and one in three children suffers from chronic malnutrition. One black South African in every four lives in absolute poverty. At the same time, South Africa faces one of the world's fastest growing HIV/AIDS epidemics. Violence, a chronic problem both in homes and in the community, is rampant. Women and girls are the main victims. In 1997 South

---

[7] Like the national legal system, indigenous justice bears the scars of the long period of war and repression, and, according to observers, cannot be said to function perfectly. (*Communication to the Council from NOVIB*, 28 February 2000.)

[8] The disaggregation could be extended further, given the distinctive effects of *apartheid* on the different ethnic communities in the country, in particular Indians and persons of mixed race. (Chidi Anselem Odinkalu, Interrights, *Communication to the Council*, March 2000.)

Africa had the highest rate of rape in the world and one of the highest rates of spousal abuse.

Under South Africa's new constitutional dispensation, the judiciary is composed of a Constitutional Court; a Supreme Court of Appeal; high courts (formerly Supreme Courts); the magistrates' courts (regional and district); and a series of special courts, including labour courts, small claims courts and courts of chiefs and headmen. The South African Police Services (SAPS) now receive human rights training and are scrutinised by several layers of internal and external oversight mechanisms, including a new Independent Complaints Directorate. Several independent commissions have also been established under Chapter 9 of the Constitution to monitor human rights and equality. They include a Human Rights Commission, a Commission for Gender Equality, and a Public Protector, among others.

Before 1994 the justice system was itself an instrument of repression and discrimination. Transforming such a system into one that serves a non-racial vision of the rule of law is an enormous challenge for South African reformers. To this end, the country has drawn up a set of detailed plans and projects to remove discrimination, enhance performance and increase access to the justice system. Realising these goals for most of the nation's people will inevitably take many years, although most of the necessary legal, policy and planning instruments are already firmly in place, and the institutions are largely established. Beneficiaries with whom we spoke said human rights assistance has played an indispensable role in this work. Ensuring that these new institutions and plans deliver services and redress to the long-excluded majority is the next challenge for South Africa and its development partners.

Three: **HUMAN RIGHTS AND DEVELOPMENT –
BRIDGING THE DIVIDE**

Human rights assistance is essentially a form of development aid that is substantively based upon international human rights standards. As such, it bridges what have been viewed as two fields of study and activity: human rights and development. A recurrent theme in many of our interviews was the need for better communication and collaboration between those involved in these two fields. This will present its own challenges in every case, but raises particular sensitivities in the context of justice reform. Some donors, for example, tend to view work in the justice sector as different – more sensitive – than support to other development sectors, which they say are less "political" and more "humanitarian". Some beneficiaries (especially human rights organisations) worry that such a distinction causes donors to act inconsistently on human rights issues. In particular, they criticise donors who choose not to speak out against governments that abuse human rights, in order to protect their aid programmes.

Still others believe that development and human rights are unrelated, even mutually exclusive activities which should be separated operationally as well as conceptually. This view is quite widely held, even if support for it is shrinking. One of those we interviewed said, for example: "Human rights are fundamentally a luxury of the advanced democracies. Emphasising the rule of law and democracy is expensive, and wasteful in poor countries." The speaker is a junior official in a leading donor organisation.

If practitioners of human rights and development are joined today in theoretical and practical debate, until recently no major donor had integrated human rights into its aid programmes and policies. None had embraced a rights-based approach to development. Relatively few offered assistance that aimed explicitly to strengthen the rule of law or institutional respect for human rights. In general, development and human rights were discussed separately. Development was considered to have a primarily economic focus, while human rights issues were thought to fall within the domain of politics. Indeed it was for this reason that many agencies refused to provide aid to human rights as a matter of policy. Others insulated development activity from human rights activity by channelling development aid and human rights aid through different institutions. When human rights were raised in relation to development, it was often only when governments applied aid conditionality or sanctions.

NGOs were similarly divided. Donors and beneficiaries still tend to speak of "development NGOs" and "human rights NGOs". These work in different ways and engage differently with official institutions. Most development agencies are essentially pragmatic institutions; the majority have their roots in multiple small-scale community projects. They are neither bound nor intellectually inspired by detailed standards or international codes. By contrast, most human rights organisations treat such standards as fundamental to the legitimacy of their work. Their dominant tradition is a legal one, built round the codification of principles. And, whereas development NGOs frequently co-operated at project level with national governments and local officials, for international human rights NGOs independence from governments has been a crucial idea. Historically, they have been more reluctant to co-operate with governments that do not have a good human rights record. International human rights NGOs have been most active in holding government officials to account for non-compliance with human rights standards. They have less experience of assisting official institutions to function efficiently, for example in the justice sector. The same is true for many (though not all) national human rights NGOs.

As human rights assistance and the legal authority of human rights standards have grown, nevertheless, the benefits of linking human rights and the wider processes of development have been recognised. Development itself is increasingly seen as a broad social and political as well as economic process, and many development professionals now consider that a rights-based approach will make development efforts more effective and sustainable. Effective co-operation is not necessarily simple to achieve, however. The two traditions have markedly different methodologies, histories and preoccupations, and they relate differently to governments. It is not surprising that friction often results. According to UN officials who are involved in "mainstreaming" human rights for example, some staff in UN development agencies have strongly objected to using mandatory, rights-based language.[9] Efforts to integrate human rights into economic and social development programmes have been resisted, as have efforts to disaggregate development statistics by race, religion or ethnicity. Proposals to include categories like "personal security", "justice administration" and "political participation" in development planning are debated intensely.

The beneficiaries we interviewed, whether they worked in government or in NGOs, generally appealed for an approach that recognises the links between different areas of economic and social development and integrates human rights throughout.

Poverty, under-development and justice
The link between poverty and under-development and a poorly-functioning justice system is an obvious one. In our discussions officials often underlined the central role of poverty in frustrating development of the justice sector. Justice officials pointed to the link between poverty and judicial corruption. Police and prison officials told us that lack of resources prevented them from implementing UN standards regarding detention or the use of force. One Ministry of Interior official

[9] UN development agencies are currently working with the Office of the High Commissioner for Human Rights to integrate human rights in all their operational programmes: this process is called "mainstreaming".

in Cambodia summed up the relationship this way: "We have but one enemy today: poverty – from which all other problems stem. This includes the weakness of the justice system and abuses that occur there. Even if the system is over-staffed, the low level of resources means that officials are under-skilled, underpaid, and under equipped."

Of course, low salaries and inadequate resources do not justify continuing abuse. Corruption and violent abuses of authority may also be found in well-resourced judicial systems. Nevertheless, their influence is significant. Indeed, adequate remuneration for judges is considered important enough to have been included in the UN Basic Principles on the Independence of the Judiciary. While other factors come into play, corruption is undoubtedly fed and facilitated by poverty.

South African beneficiaries made the same connection between poverty and weak justice. One NGO representative said, for example: "Human rights in the justice system costs money. The old system of repression was comparatively cheap." South Africa faces huge social problems of crime. It is also trying to manage a new constitutional and legal order, which has established an unprecedented array of independent commissions and oversight mechanisms. Those we met viewed these as necessary if South Africa is to move from a system that denied the majority access to justice, to one that will ensure the rule of law – but the new system is expensive.

Measuring success and failure

Aid presumes need. Organisations that have well defined programmes, sustainable resources and adequate budgets, sufficient capacity, well trained staff, helpful environments and stable and well-functioning institutions around them, do not need foreign aid or external advice. Of course, a supply of aid does not necessarily reduce need successfully. Many independent factors influence success or failure, and it is difficult both to set targets and objectively measure impact. Some aid providers find it is even more difficult to sustain programmes when failures in implementation result in continuing human rights abuses.

International aid in the field of human rights developed precisely to assist governments to meet their obligations under relevant treaties and declarations. Performance and success were thought to be more easily measurable – by the degree to which assisted governments complied with international standards in the area concerned. However, since human rights assistance is (like other forms of development aid) especially required by institutions that operate imperfectly and in an unhelpful environment, it follows that, in almost all cases, such assistance will not immediately lift performance to international standards – and certainly will not do so perfectly. In this respect, when it comes to measuring impact and success, aid programmes in the justice assistance face most of the same intransigent problems as anti-poverty development projects or humanitarian relief. Measurements of effectiveness and success need to take account of capacity and context. In practice, it is not enough to judge the usefulness or performance of such programmes merely by reference to international standards, and it is in any event impossible to do so in the short term. Judgements need to be calibrated against what is possible and what is reasonable ambition. This, however, is a hard reality to face when working in the justice sector, where "failures" can be expressed in terms of torture, summary executions, brutality and impunity. It is easier (though not necessarily honest) to explain failures to grow crops, provide potable water, or reduce poverty as tragic acts of nature. In the justice sector, critics will ask, can failures relate to anything but the acts of men and women?

A rights-based approach to development

Development and donor agencies talk increasingly of a *rights-based approach* to development (though few implement it in practice). We view a rights-based approach as one that defines the objectives of aid in terms of rights (the right to health, to education, to food, etc). It begins with the identification of a particular right, and defines the normative and practical content of that right with reference to international and national standards and jurisprudence. It names particular claim-holders (and their entitlements) and corresponding duty-holders (and their obligations), increasing accountability by moving away from an approach that is essentially charitable towards one that offers legally enforceable entitlements. This implies the existence of adequate laws, policies, institutions and mechanisms to deliver on the entitlement, and of mechanisms to redress violations or denials. A rights-based approach also necessarily gives particular attention to issues of discrimination and the situation of poor and excluded groups. It therefore requires disaggregation of development data by race, religion, ethnicity and so on (in addition to already standard gender-disaggregation).

Most important, the necessary focus of a rights-based approach should be on those who stand to benefit (or lose) – those whose rights are in jeopardy and need strengthening. Human rights belong not to governments, to donors, or to international agencies, but to people. People, therefore, directly through their advocates, and collectively through organisations of civil society and elected representatives, must not only participate in but be able to direct the course of reforms aimed at strengthening their claims to and realisation of human rights. This means consulting them, including them in decision-making, and involving them in setting targets and monitoring and evaluating progress.

Some assistance agencies, having embraced a "people-centred" approach to development, have become increasingly comfortable with this notion. For others, however, the implications are threatening, challenging both the foundations of the way they provide aid, and the balance of interests that have been built up around the past half century of aid. There are many partners in the development equation, and only so much "authority" to go around. If more is to be given to the beneficiaries, from whom is it to be taken away? Donors? Governments? Foreign NGOs? Convenors of regional "strategies" and fora? UN treaty bodies and special rapporteurs? Tax payers in donor countries? It is easy to recognise the authority of people on the ground in policy statements and speeches. Empowering them – even against one's own interest – is far more difficult.

Beneficiaries and a rights-based approach

A rights-based approach to development has implications for the relationship between donors and beneficiaries. In the context of this approach, we should not lose sight of the fact that the ultimate "beneficiaries" of justice sector reform are not governments, official institutions or NGOs, but individuals who need legal protection. Nevertheless, NGO and official beneficiaries generally stand in a closer position to those individuals than do donor agencies. A domestic NGO can claim to represent the views of victims, and a government (at least where it is democratically elected) does speak on behalf of the population it governs. Therefore, prioritising beneficiary views, showing a genuine commitment to respecting those views and giving them due authority in the design and implementation of human rights aid, is itself part of a rights-based approach. The approach implies that the legitimacy of decision-making mechanisms must be judged, at least in part, by their proximity to the people to be benefited. A rights-based approach is process-based, rather than overly reliant on approaches that are imported from abroad. It aims to ensure genuine local involvement in development, so that aid is responsive to the perceived needs, problems and aspirations of the population being served. Local accountability is important, as is respect for the authority of domestic reform constituencies

A concern we heard in the course of this study is that, in matters of human rights assistance, some of the beneficiaries (especially those in official institutions like police, prisons, and courts) are in fact human rights violators, and that one should therefore be cautious in advocating beneficiary empowerment. There are two answers to this concern. First, serious human rights assistance programmes to the justice sector should begin with international human rights standards, and should presume their universality and applicability. A beneficiary perspective that is racist or sexist or that rejects fair trial guarantees, for example, would not be endorsed under this approach. Nor would approaches that ignore vulnerable groups, or trample on rights in the name of majoritarian trends, meet this test.

Second, we have defined beneficiaries to include both government institutions and civil society. Also, the ultimate beneficiaries are of course the general domestic population who stand to benefit from reforms. Empowering beneficiaries does not mean endorsing official propaganda or defending the tyranny of the majority. Hence the importance (discussed more fully below) of including civil society as well as official institutions in a comprehensive view of the justice sector.

For some, this presents a contradiction. Most development specialists are now comfortable with the concept of domestic (beneficiary) ownership. Human rights professionals are at home with the notion that international standards are paramount. Some from both groups will think that it may be necessary to choose between international standards and local legitimacy. In practice, we believe these two approaches can be reconciled. They are the two complementary sides of the human rights and development coin. Human rights assistance is about advancing international standards through development co-operation. This is done through partnerships established expressly to that end. Thus, between donor and beneficiary the authority for reforms rests with the beneficiary. At the same time, to achieve respect for human rights, both sides need to observe international standards. Aid programmes that do not respect international standards cannot properly be considered human rights assistance.

Donor constraints

Recognising the centrality of the beneficiary perspective to attempts at improving aid may, however, be only half the battle. Also crucial to a critical review is an understanding of key donor constraints in the field. Human rights assistance to the justice sector presents particular challenges to donors seeking to support meaningful reform and development. The impact of the political will factor, and the difficulties associated with locating, measuring and encouraging a commitment to reform, are discussed below. Even where commitment is less of an issue, limited domestic capacity, in the context of dramatic justice sector reforms, often restricts donor efforts to maximise domestic ownership and participation. At the same time, the sector includes a number of institutions (courts, human rights commissions, etc.) which are independent under the law. Reforms cannot be imposed politically on such institutions, and standard donor approaches to advice, funding, and even communications are not always appropriate either. Some have also suggested that donors must sometimes tread more lightly here, as the institutions of the justice sector (courts, police, prisons), are (or are seen to be) situated closer to the core of national sovereignty than are hospitals, schools, roads or dams.

For bilateral donors (and the EU), assistance is never insulated entirely from questions of foreign policy. What is more, responsible donors do (and should) make efforts to avoid underwriting repression, camouflaging false reform processes, or acting in complicity with abusive governments. Resources being limited, such donors will also feel the pressure of competing development demands from other sectors and from other countries. Nor do donors generally have the same level of experience and capacity to provide human rights assistance, or justice sector support, as they do with other kinds of development assistance. The work is necessarily long-term, lacks reliable indicators, and does not lend itself easily to traditional assistance methodologies. Few donor agencies have sufficient numbers of personnel on their staff with expertise in international human rights standards, and the ability to translate these standards into national institutions and laws, such that experts are often able to offer only comparative national models, often of limited relevance to local realities. Finally, donor engagement in the justice sector will almost always elicit some form of response and critique from the public both in the beneficiary country, and in the donor country. When public opinion in both is harmonious, donor choices are easier. When they are not, what is a donor to do?

Four: THRESHOLD ISSUES –
WHEN TO PROVIDE ASSISTANCE AND TO WHOM?

Much of what we learned in the course of this study suggests that human rights assistance should be planned and managed in a more strategic fashion, and the partnership between donor and beneficiary should be strengthened and made more equal. These issues are discussed in later chapters. Our interviews also threw up questions and debates, often of a more political nature, about when it is appropriate to provide (or withdraw) human rights assistance, and to whom such assistance should be given. In this chapter we discuss such threshold issues.

When to engage (or disengage)?

The discourse of the first fifty years of the modern human rights movement has been marked by a conceptual framework of mutually-exclusive alternatives: government versus civil society; public security versus civil liberties; economic and social rights versus civil and political rights; monitoring and condemnation versus technical assistance and constructive engagement. In this world of exclusive choices, the role of human rights activists was correspondingly evident: expose abuses, and demand accountability for violators and justice for their victims. The dominant strategy, at least for NGOs, has thus been one of public pressure, directed to forcing governments to respect rights by embarrassing them through exposure of abuses. This paradigm has been constructed upon a number of important assumptions about the nature of human rights and requirements for their realisation. At its core is a liberal and somewhat *laissez faire* view of rights, according to which the state need only refrain from violations to ensure rights are realised.

Increasingly, and especially during the 1990s, human rights proponents have come to realise that negative prohibitions are not sufficient. Positive steps are equally necessary to realise the full range of rights contained in international standards. Thus, the right to adequate housing requires both that the government refrain from punitive demolitions and unlawful forced evictions, and that it take positive action to protect and deliver on the right, through well functioning courts, social welfare programmes, administrative mechanisms, and enforcement measures. Similarly, ensuring free and fair elections requires more than an absence of government interference with voters, parties and candidates. Meaningful reform and respect for human rights in the administration of justice require both a commitment to respect rights, and the physical, financial and technical means to ensure that commitment can be met. Developing countries and countries in transition may lack one, or both of these. Human rights assistance, which can contribute in either case, is therefore both about supplementing institutional resources and enhancing political commitment. The latter may be achieved by supporting organisations and institutions that monitor violations and demand reforms, and the former by strengthening a range of institutions across the functions of government. In both cases, aid seeks to accomplish its ends through the provision of loans, grants, advice, training, equipment, materials, facilities and other standard "delivery vehicles".

Is there, however, a minimum level of commitment to reform required before assistance is provided (or withdrawn), and how would it be measured? This question clearly troubles aid providers, at least when they are considering engagement with official institutions in recipient countries. Clear guidelines are elusive, but our interviews with a wide range of beneficiaries in all 4 countries, in both government and civil society, showed a strong bias towards engagement even where commitment to reform is in doubt.

There are extreme cases where beneficiaries say that human rights assistance to the government would be wasteful, even counterproductive: South Africa under *apartheid*; perhaps Bulgaria under totalitarian rule; probably Guatemala in the 1980s; certainly Cambodia under the Khmer Rouge. In sum, where the ideology and policies of a government conflict explicitly with international human rights standards, providing aid of this kind to official institutions of the state is likely not to be appropriate.

All other cases, we were told, require careful judgement. Overly simplistic political reactions, said beneficiaries, will sooner or later jeopardise support for reform and will therefore be counter-productive. Countries are not monolithic, nor are governments within countries, or institutions within governments, or individuals within those institutions. Human rights assistance can not only strengthen political commitment to reform, it can create that commitment where it is absent. In sum, the calculation to be made is complex and should not be considered in terms of a simple binary alternative.

Beneficiaries saw many opportunities to provide human rights assistance usefully even where the political commitment of governments is in doubt. Support reformist institutions in conservative governments. Support individual reformers and pockets of reform in institutions resistant to change. Work with the "demand side" of reform: civil society, national human rights institutions, and reformist parliamentarians. Where necessary, direct aid to official institutions through national NGOs. The important thing, said beneficiaries, is to engage. Some donors have certainly adopted this approach. A principal donor to the justice sector in one country advised that: "It is not wasteful to build capacity in times of low political will or limited freedom of action. So long as that capacity exists, and is ready to be mobilised when the opportunity arises, then aid has done its job."

Beneficiaries also said that donors should not too easily jump to "safe programmes" (without political risk for them) in cases where a government's commitment to reform is doubtful. (See the section on "safe aid" below.) If this becomes the norm, as seems to have happened to some degree in all of the focus countries, reform of official institutions will not progress. Some donors, we learned, tend almost automatically to support alternative structures (alternative dispute resolution, national human rights commissions, NGO mechanisms) before attempting to engage with the regular justice institutions. Other donors, however, have continued to engage with official institutions. Representatives of one of these told us that it is not realistic to wait for ideal political conditions. Referring to Cambodia, he said it is often better to "dig in and try to help build things project by project".

In some cases, human rights assistance has been used to circumvent obstructionist forces in the system. South African beneficiaries in at least two official institutions used donor projects and funding to implement institutional reform programmes. By these means they could avoid points of resistance they had encountered earlier (using regular national budgets). South Africans had differing views of this practice. Some saw it as a useful way to circumvent political obstacles. Others wondered whether the practice was not simply delaying inevitable confrontations, in an essentially artificial manoeuvre that could cause more problems in the long term. Was it not better to confront points of resistance directly, rather than isolate them in pockets of resentment?

Whatever South African beneficiaries ultimately decide on this issue, it raises a number of important questions relating to reform and political commitment. One of these is the importance of individuals within the institutions being reformed. Success, we were told, can sometimes turn on a single reformer or a single resister. Aid providers therefore "need to know which is which". This requires true dialogue, listening and learning. One official in South Africa recalled how a donor-appointed project steering committee, assembled without appropriate care, itself became an obstruction to reform. "The donor followed a checklist, appointing so many black members, so many white members, so many women, and so on. They did not consult enough, and what they failed to take into account was that some of these were in fact extremely conservative individuals, opposed to many of the reforms to be implemented."

Some beneficiaries in Bulgaria told us that donors had more rather than less reason to become involved when government institutions were insufficiently committed to reform. Bulgarian judges told us that weak commitment was the strongest reason for donors to engage and stay engaged. Noting that the reform process faced tremendous inertia from decades of the old system, one judge said "there will always be politicians and others who oppose reforms. International support helps to push those reforms through".[10]

After the violent events of July 1997, donors in Cambodia cut foreign assistance to the country. Human rights assistance was not spared. The Human Rights Commission of the National Assembly, the judiciary and even some human rights NGOs suffered partial or complete severance of aid. "What was the message?"

asked one observer. "We are cutting off support for the rule of law, because we support the rule of law?" Both NGO and official beneficiaries told us that they viewed the cut-off as inappropriate and unhelpful, based more on narrow foreign policy goals than on a measured judgement of what would best advance the rule of law. Even those who believed that sanctions were a necessary response told us that this should not apply to technical assistance and training directed to the justice system. Said one: "When [donors] disengaged unilaterally after July 1997, they damaged reform partners and the reform effort. This was unacceptable."

Ups and downs – the Guatemala experience

In the 1980s and early 1990s, there was particularly heated debate over whether Guatemala should receive human rights assistance. Following the installation of a nominally civilian government in 1986 and the establishment of a human rights ombudsman (*Procurador de los Derechos Humanos*), both the United States (USAID) and the UN (the advisory services programme, as mandated by the Commission on Human Rights) decided to provide human rights assistance to the official sector. Guatemalan and international human rights groups cried foul. They argued that gross violations of human rights were continuing and that these aid programmes diverted attention from the atrocities and from official responsibilities for them. They further argued that the power structure was ideologically committed to racism and repression and that suppression of fundamental human rights was not accidental. The problems were political, not technical, and the appropriate response was political pressure, not aid.

In the end, the donors concerned came to the same conclusions. The USAID programme was terminated a few years later "in the face of an absolute lack of political will" and the UN programme limited much of its support to the office of the human rights ombudsman. Other donors supported NGOs only. This experience indelibly marked the justice sector in Guatemala. Major donors did not resume support to official institutions (other than the ombudsman) until peace accords were signed and new reforms launched in 1994. Guatemalan human rights specialists told us this was right because "no real reforms were possible before the peace accords brought new openings and a degree of verifiable political will. Before that, the only genuine options were protest and resistance". At the same time, they recognised the crucial role played by the ombudsman. Whatever the doubts of observers when this institution was established (during one of the war's bloodiest periods), Guatemalans recognise that it developed a

---

[10] A number of others also emphasised this aspect. Amin Mekki Medani, who heads the Office of the United Nations High Commissioner for Human Rights in Palestine, observed that "where there is a serious lack of political will in countries that view democratic institutions and human rights principles as a threat to their political regimes... human rights assistance is most needed". He believes that by engaging assistance providers can "help in creating political will", not through classic conditionality (which hurts the people but does not deter the regimes), but by "exercising leverage for change". (*Communication to the Council*, 9 March 2000.)

momentum of its own. Most believed that this was due to the high personal profile of the person appointed to the job and the close involvement of international donors in its operation. As an official (albeit independent) institution, it acquired exceptional credibility.

When the peace accords were signed, human rights assistance returned to Guatemala's official sector in 1994, and especially in 1996 when a Comprehensive Agreement on Human Rights was approved under UN supervision and verification. Plans were drawn up, co-ordination bodies established, and new projects launched. Some $80 million in aid was made available to the justice sector and, in addition to expanded projects by both the UN human rights programme and USAID (the original providers), new projects were launched by MINUGUA (the UN operation in the country), UNDP, the EU, the World Bank, the Inter-American Development Bank and other donors. The peace agreements themselves became a barometer of political will, the platform upon which reform work would be built. Guatemala's political will problem was solved. Almost.

When a national referendum on constitutional reforms delivered a "no" vote in 1999, some donors reportedly interpreted the result as a step back from political reform, and delayed aid to the justice sector. Some donors had expressly linked aid packages to progress in the peace process. With the "no" vote, some projects were reconsidered and other projects delayed. Such decisions, apparently, rested on two assumptions. The first was that the "no" vote represented a rejection of political reform. The second was the notion that stopping aid is sometimes more influential than giving it. Yet, most of those to whom we spoke believed that the referendum result did not signal a refusal to reform but was the result of a mix of factors – including the complex nature of the ballot (some fifty separate reforms were included), low turnout by voters, limited support for the ruling party, lost momentum after the peace accords, low public trust in official institutions by the (majority) indigenous communities, and poor voter education and information. As for the second assumption, few of the beneficiaries we met considered it was an appropriate approach in this context. Most, including NGOs, believed that donors should remain engaged with official institutions, working with reformers to advance the human rights development process.

One key question in such situations is how to identify reformers. Some donors in Guatemala have followed progressive strategies, first supporting only NGOs, then supporting the ombudsman, and finally and gradually engaging with the official sector. In the official sector, the human rights ombudsman and bodies co-ordinating judicial reform have been the preferred choice. Other institutions are viewed as more difficult. Officers of the six-thousand strong Guatemalan Bar Association, for example, consider that they and their organisation have been excluded from help during the reform process. The legal profession is generally viewed as a conservative force in Guatemalan society and many consider it to be a pocket of resistance to genuine legal reform. The various justice reform bodies, and the donors that support them, have, we were told, kept their distance. Lawyers, however, wondered how reform of the system could be conceived and implemented without the involvement of one of its key constituencies. We asked officers of the Bar Association whether the Bar should be viewed as a natural constituency for, or a conservative impediment to, legal reforms. "It is both," we were told. "Every institution contains reformers and resisters, conservatives and advocates for change. The Bar is no different. It has been a conservative force, but its membership is increasingly diverse. Today, there are many in the organisation who are not only committed to reforms, but engaged in them in their personal capacity." Members also pointed to the range of legal skills available within the Bar and their relevance to the work to be done. Given that some major donors are providing human rights assistance to a very broad range of institutions (including the military), some questioned the wisdom of excluding a body that clearly plays a role central to the functioning of the justice system.

Seen through the donor lens, however, legitimate questions about the challenge of political commitment remain. We have noted that, broadly speaking, recipients agreed that aid should not be provided in extreme cases where official policy is expressly contrary to human rights requirements. In less extreme cases, however, when is it appropriate to cut aid in response to weak official commitment to reform? Donors have a responsibility to avoid complicity with repressive governments. Yet, is it sensible to abandon reformers in the country at precisely the moment when they most need support? Clearly, no automatic formula can resolve such dilemmas. Beneficiaries (including NGOs) did not want donors to delay aid to the justice sector following the failure of the constitutional reform referendum in Guatemala. They were critical of those donors who cut assistance to Cambodia following the coup of July 1997. Beneficiaries seemed to set a high threshold for freezing this type of assistance on such grounds.

There do seem to be good reasons to insulate human rights assistance from premature cancellation. First, the cost of cutting aid to reform (and reformers) can be high, and, in the absence of reliable indicators by which to measure commitment to reform, safe judgements in unclear cases (probably the majority) are difficult at best. Secondly, transitional periods are always marked by ups and downs in the reform process. These fluctuations, if coupled with a low threshold for cut-offs, would make sustained support for reforms impossible in almost every case. Third, it is arguably inconsistent for donors to punish abuse of human rights by cancelling programmes that exist to strengthen human rights protection.

Nor are arguments about aid fungibility (i.e., that aid to the justice sector allows the government to spend its money on other non-human rights activities) as convincing with human rights assistance as with other types of aid. The amounts committed to this sector are relatively small. Most of the human rights assistance provided to the justice sector was in the form of less fungible support like training and technical advice, rather than grants, equipment, or material aid. What is more, beneficiaries with whom we met doubted in most cases that governments would attach priority attention to some of these activities in the absence of external support. Finally, significant portions of aid to the sector go directly to NGOs, independent commissions, oversight mechanisms, and the judiciary – none of which would clearly appear to be fair targets for donor attempts to sanction the government.

In the end, the beneficiaries said that the best approach donors could take, when faced with difficult choices, was to ask the beneficiaries themselves about whether aid should be continued or cut. Decisions on such questions should, they suggest, only be made after consulting independent actors and organisations in the country who have direct knowledge about (and greatest stake in) the reform process. In the end, donors may indeed arrive at different conclusions than those they consult, but the legitimacy of their decisions will ultimately rest on the degree to which the donor has properly taken into account local views on the matter.

Monitoring and engaging

Of course, one potential problem of assistance to official institutions arises when those institutions (police, prisons, etc.) do not immediately reform but rather (and as is more likely) continue to engage in abusive behaviour. We asked several donors whether their approach to failures in the justice system differed from their approach to failures or deficiencies in other sectors. Most did deal differently with justice. Officials said that the key difference was the "political" character of the justice system, compared to health, education, and so on. Some therefore took a "less direct approach" when they raised matters of concern to them, and others avoided doing so. Some told us that straightforward interventions with government were possible but should be confidential.

Some beneficiaries, especially human rights NGOs, were dissatisfied by such approaches. They thought that an over-cautious approach reinforced the view within government that these issues were "sensitive", and "political". Others argued that a "silent" approach reduced transparency in an area vital to the public interest. One NGO representative charged that "when donors are inconsistent in their support for human rights, they damage efforts toward their promotion and protection". One criticism was that some donors "fund NGOs to monitor, investigate and take risks on the one hand, and then remain silent when we are threatened by officials for those very same activities". Another worried that some aid providers fund organisations that comment on draft laws and institutional proposals "and then remain silent when these proposals are ignored".

The perception that donors are unwilling to criticise or speak out when abuses continue raises another point, namely the traditional tension between human rights activities that aim to monitor abuses (and denounce them) and activities that help reform the system. It is often thought that if you provide assistance for reform, your ability to speak out is limited, for example because doing so will lead the government to cease co-operation (or vice-versa). Fears of this kind partially explain why NGOs engaged in traditional human rights monitoring activities, at least at the international level, have been sceptical about human rights assistance work.

In fact, meaningful human rights assistance in a country is not possible without monitoring the human rights situation. If the purpose of justice sector reform is to bring policies and practice into line with international human rights standards, then projects must be able to assess when current policy and practice fall below those standards. Reforms cannot be developed and implemented without identifying what needs to be reformed. Monitoring and assistance are not therefore antagonistic activities but mutually reinforcing to one another. In our discussions, this was generally recognised by all types of beneficiaries. No serious programme of aid could contribute to justice reform without monitoring. Evaluation of a project will necessarily involve monitoring the institutional context. Post-project evaluations will try to look at impact. Of necessity, such monitoring and evaluation would have to look at continuing human rights violations, and, in this sense, aid-related monitoring would be similar to traditional human rights monitoring.

The real controversy, of course, is around the question of whether *public* reporting on continuing abuses is the best course of action for those providing assistance. There are differences of approach among both donors and beneficiaries. AUSAID's major criminal justice assistance project in Cambodia, for example, operates in the context of an agreed approach of confidentiality. Most official bilateral donors usually operate more or less in this way.

The debate about engaging in assistance and/or reporting publicly on abuses is different for inter-governmental agencies like the UN (or regional organisations like the Council of Europe or the Organisation of American States - OAS). Such organisations are expected both to assist governments *and* report publicly on the human rights situation in different countries. In Guatemala, for example, MINUGUA both provides assistance and monitors abuses (including detailed public reporting). MINUGUA's findings in monitoring abuses are used, *inter alia*, to inform its assistance activities. Similarly, in Cambodia, the Office of the United Nations High Commissioner for Human Rights (OHCHR) is mandated, with the UN's Special Representative, to carry out monitoring, investigations, public reporting and technical co-operation in the country (under a series of General Assembly and Commission on Human Rights resolutions, and an agreement with the government). OHCHR has carried out hundreds of assistance activities since it opened following the departure of UNTAC, including training of government officials, advice on draft laws, and strengthening of government institutions. Nevertheless, until now, most media attention (within the country and abroad) has focused on the investigative and public reporting side of its work, and this has created a false perception that investigation represents the bulk of the Office's activities.

Problems arise for intergovernmental organisations when, as a consequence of political trade-offs and bargaining, the provision of assistance and advisory services is mandated *instead* of public reporting. Governments that face criticism, for example in the UN Commission on Human Rights, will agree to a UN assistance programme in order to deflect pressure for what is perceived as a more intrusive "monitoring" regime (such as the appointment of a Special Rapporteur). Of course, the effect of such arrangements is to discredit the assistance programme.

These tensions may reflect historical (and perhaps well-founded) prejudices about human rights assistance and the weakness of some assistance programmes, rather than any real assessment of the intrusive implications of monitoring versus those of assistance. Properly understood, serious assistance programmes are potentially far more "intrusive", and operate closer to the pressure points of state sovereignty than any external monitoring regime. Traditional monitoring simply identifies and announces abuses. Serious assistance programmes, in addition to identifying abuses, also propose solutions, and intervene directly in a country's courts, police, prisons, political systems and a host of other governmental functions. In some cases, foreign advisors may have more influence in the structure and functioning of public institutions than voters, or some of the officials they vote for. If officials of an abusive government seem eager to conclude an assistance agreement in place of a monitoring mission, they may be expecting "a few harmless seminars". If that is in fact the donor's intention as well, then the programme will certainly get the reputation it deserves. Unfortunately, it is reformers, and reform, that lose most in such cases.

Providing assistance should not, therefore, rule out involvement in monitoring and public reporting. Political trade-offs between monitoring and assistance should be resisted. The UN must be able to do both, or risk the credibility of its assistance programmes. The same is true for other intergovernmental bodies that have a mandate to report publicly on human rights. Government donors, on the other hand, might argue that their programmes proceed more effectively when criticisms are made in confidence to the government. There is no easy answer here. The NGO beneficiaries we spoke to generally felt donors should not shy away from public criticism, and a number of government officials agreed that such criticism could be helpful. Ultimately, much depends on the situation in the country concerned and the donor's mandate and mission. On the whole, nevertheless, we lean towards saying that, unless there is very strong case for confidentiality, donors should support principles of transparency and accountability, and should allow for public reporting of their criticisms.

Who to engage? Institution building in the official sector

Those we interviewed said that donors sometimes fail to engage fully with official justice sector institutions because they do not have confidence in a government's commitment to reform or fear being associated themselves with abusive institutions. Some donors also decide, given limited budgets, to assist NGOs committed to reform rather than government agencies with weak reform credentials. Beneficiaries criticised such an approach. They argued, correctly, that justice administration is a state function, and that the police, prisons, courts and prosecutors are state institutions. Meaningful institution-building in the justice sector cannot avoid or circumvent aid to state institutions. Yet, some donors do precisely this. It is true that non-state bodies can deliver services in a number of areas like housing or health-care programmes (though it may not always be advisable to encourage them to do so). They can advocate and campaign to encourage reform and monitor abuses. They cannot, however, hold trials, make arrests, pass laws, or imprison people. Institution building in the official sector is an essential dimension of improved human rights protection.

Interestingly, the leading national non-governmental human rights organisations in all four of the focus countries we visited have consistently engaged with official institutions – advising judges, training police and prison officials, commenting on legislative drafts, and so on. Beneficiaries argued that this proved donors should adopt a more sophisticated and measured approach towards assistance to governments and support for official institutions. A decision to build closer ties with official institutions does not, of course, remove constraints on such relationships, including official corruption, political influence, or military intimidation. It advocates instead developing a strategy of co-operation and solidarity with reformers and reformist institutions and organisations to resist and counter such problems.

Cambodia is a case in point. "Cambodia still has no rule of law, and no strong institutions: only personalities and personal power." This observation by a Khmer human rights activist is a concise statement of the situation, and equally a judgement about where human rights aid should be directed. The same remark might have been made a decade ago and this points to a weakness of human rights assistance so far. While donors have put many resources into the monitoring of abuse, government and non-governmental beneficiaries repeatedly said that donors had failed to provide sufficient assistance to official institutions in the justice sector. Though they were acutely aware of the inhibiting effects of almost continuous political instability, and the doubtful commitment of the government to human rights, Cambodians insisted that donor reluctance in this area had resulted in lost opportunities. "Donors say 'the system is hopeless, so we cannot support it'. They lack clear thinking. If it is broken, help fix it," was one comment we heard. In a discussion about the strong monitoring capacity now evident in Cambodian human rights organisations, and the weak implementing capacity of the official institutions, one donor representative noted that: "Thanks to an unbalanced approach to assistance, Cambodia now has NGOs with much capacity, and a justice system with little."

A Ministry of Justice official in Cambodia summed up his office's frustration by saying: "Donors demand reforms, then are silent when we ask them to help". Justice officials are well aware of the enormity of the challenge facing the justice system. They have repeatedly approached donors seeking to conclude assistance agreements. To little avail, they say. "Decades of war have reduced the justice system to almost nothing. It operates today only at a very low level. Officials and judges lack basic competence, principal laws and procedures have still not been developed, facilities are dilapidated, courts are held in broken down houses. Working conditions, salaries, facilities, all work against professionalisation, competence and integrity." Nor do local officials (uniformly) ignore the importance of political commitment. On the contrary, some officials to whom we spoke raised this issue themselves. They argued it was an additional justification for providing aid to the sector. "Justice support from donors is crucial. They must know that some in government see [a strong justice system] as a double-edged sword, that can come back to cut the power of police, military, and political parties. Cambodia's partners must help to keep up the momentum." Another official illustrated the direct link between a weak justice system and impunity: "We think the number of criminal convictions is far too low, because many people who commit crimes are not convicted. The problem of impunity, fed in part by corruption, and in part by a weak justice system, is widespread. The people feel very insecure."

Before 1997, official organisations in the Cambodian justice sector received some assistance from Japan, Australia, the Office of the High Commissioner for Human Rights (OHCHR), and the International Human Rights Law Group. Most was directed to judges, although some also went to lawyers groups.[11] By the end of 1999, the only major programmes were those of OHCHR and Australia (AUSAID). AUSAID's experience is instructive. Its Criminal Justice Assistance Project (CJAP) took what some called a courageous (and others a foolish) path by engaging with official institutions in 1997, when others would not. It has sustained its engagement since then. Most of the beneficiaries to whom we spoke now agree that CJAP has proved worthwhile. It has already led to the implementation of several "nuts and bolts" improvements in the judicial police, prisons and courts. "We look at the problems together with our partners, and then come up with

[11] For example, the International Human Rights Law Group, the American Bar Association and the Bar of Lyon provided support to the Bar Association, and Novib assisted the NGO Legal Aid of Cambodia.

solutions. To lessen the risk of abusive use of force in prisons, for example, we reviewed the procedures, and found that, [for situations of unrest or fleeing offenders] the rule was to shoot first in the air, and then in the back. We didn't just help revise the rules – we provided whistles."[12] The project has provided advice and training, supported the development of manuals, handbooks, and guidelines (including a Courts Handbook, a Police Operational Manual, Investigation Procedures, Prisons Procedure Manual, Standard Guidelines for Cambodian Prisons, and a Prisoner Health Manual); has simplified record keeping procedures; and has helped with construction and equipment. The practical, working level approach of the project has allowed it to achieve useful progress in spite of the inevitable ups and downs of the political situation. Whatever the perceived level of political will in higher quarters, project staff say that co-operation at the working level has been excellent, and that beneficiaries have demonstrated a "thirst for learning new skills and a willingness to implement new procedures".

Cambodian beneficiaries also said that most of the assistance provided to police, prisons, judges and others since 1992, has been in the form of *ad hoc* training courses. Very few activities have focused on building institutional capacity – such as training trainers rather than running single seminars. The experience of Cambodia's police illustrates this narrow focus. For all of the support provided through UNTAC, and the training conducted between 1992 and 1997, humane and effective policing failed to develop. Nor was training institutionalised. The police were told (generally) what the standards were, but lacked the means to apply them. They received no assistance to draft standing orders; to help develop a permanent national curriculum; to develop a police school; to purchase equipment; to write public information materials; to design guidelines on community policing; to improve detention facilities; or to establish internal oversight mechanisms.[13]

Transition in South Africa presents other challenges to official institutions in the justice sector. South African officials working in the police, courts, and prisons must manage the reform process while confronting significant pressure caused by rising crime and public insecurity. Until recently, for example, the police were organised, trained, directed and maintained as an institution of repression. Their job was, essentially, to enforce *apartheid* policy and defend the order that it

---

[12] The primary aim was to give officials an alternative which was safer, cheaper, more respectful of human rights, and less likely to draw criticism, according to project officials.

[13] Koy Neam of the Asia Foundation in Cambodia underscored the practical areas of potential police assistance that relate more to capacity than to will. He notes that: "Cambodian police, due to lack of skills in... investigations (e.g., scientific methodology or interrogation skills) resort to violence to extract a confession. [I]n many cases, that confession is used as a basis for conviction." (*Communication to the Council*, March 2000.)

represented. They must now internalise new rules of police conduct, relate to a broad spectrum of new monitoring mechanisms, respond to the expectations of a population terrified by rising crime, and cope with the fact that police are themselves being killed in record numbers. Operational resources, say the authorities, are stretched to the limit. Most goes to salaries, leaving little to upgrade equipment and facilities and even less to ensure that human rights training and other reform interventions are effective. In these circumstances, say beneficiaries inside and out of the police, the extent to which the police emerge from the transition as a "human rights-friendly" institution will depend to an important degree on donor commitment. Some donors have supported community policing and human rights training for the police. Many South Africans view such programmes as model initiatives, with enormous potential for transforming South Africa's model of law enforcement. Though it is too early to evaluate their success, observers believe some lessons are already emerging. One is that, because generous start-up assistance was not sustained, the benefits of an impressive human rights training programme did not trickle down through the ranks. For the same reason, a creative community policing initiative has also disappointed. Donors, said NGOs and police in South Africa, should sustain support to the official sector until good pilot programmes become established and sustainable. For effective institution building, and given that donors have limited resources, it may be preferable for donors to support fewer initiatives in a sustained manner rather than run many small projects with many partners.

In Guatemala, both NGOs and government institutions seek more support to help them transform the official institutions of justice. Guatemala's history of gross violations of rights, the failure of numerous efforts to reform, and the fact that most (though not all) donors long focused their aid on NGOs as a result, has created conditions in which "people know their rights, and know how to demand them, but the system cannot deliver on those demands".

Bulgarian NGOs and officials also agree that donors must assist official institutions in the justice system if reform is to be sustained. With its heavy focus on European integration since 1997, the government has been increasingly willing to implement reform. Reform advocates said this should be exploited. NGOs agreed, but added that human rights support to official justice institutions should in every case be directed to reform processes (not just institutions), should be accompanied by clear public information about the nature and content of programmes, and should involve NGOs.

The "safe aid" factor

Beneficiary experience suggests that donors view some forms of aid, and some kinds of beneficiaries, as somehow "safer" than others. Assistance trends in the four countries visited seem to bear this out. Judges receive more support than prisons and prosecutors. Police receive training but not defensive equipment. The result is often a reduced capacity to perform official justice functions in conformity with international standards.

Beneficiaries (and some donors) suggested that donors fear their assistance could attract bad publicity, or create political risks, should the institutions they support act abusively. Untrained guards might abuse prisoners because they are not aware of their rights, but blame will fall on the UN if it has trained them. Prison conditions are widely inhumane, but donors know they are the first to be criticised if abuses occur in a prison their aid has benefited. Police sometimes have no alternative but to use lethal force – but donors will be blamed if they have supplied riot control equipment that is used abusively against peaceful protestors. Beneficiaries recognised these fears, but most considered the long term benefits of aid outweigh the risks of political exposure, and that the alternatives are unacceptable – untrained guards, dilapidated prisons, uncontrolled use of firearms, unreformed prosecutors, etc.

In Cambodia, prosecutors, prisons and the Interior Ministry have received relatively little human rights assistance. There are a few notable exceptions, including advisory support from OHCHR and the AUSAID CJAP project. Cambodian NGOs have provided most of the assistance received by prosecutors in the form of seminars and training courses. Prosecutors said that donors have not asked them to assess their needs. They said that requests for assistance to help them train prosecutors and establish oversight and control mechanisms have had no response. Ministry of Interior officials recounted a similar experience. They benefited from some training provided by local human rights groups but had received no direct support from donors. OHCHR and local NGOs have offered some training courses to prison staff in Cambodia, and they receive increasing levels of support from AUSAID. Nevertheless, they have not had significant help from any major assistance programme. Even so, aid seems to have had some measurable impact. Summing up the situation, NGOs and prison officials agreed that treatment has improved since 1992, while conditions have not. "So far, we have received only limited humanitarian assistance, and some occasional legal assistance for prisoners," prison authorities told us. "The training provided to prisoners and guards by the NGOs and by OHCHR since 1992 has had a positive impact, however. In the beginning, the prisoners had never heard of the concept of 'defenders'. Today, they know that they exist, and that they have a right to be assisted by them."

As for treatment, shackles have been removed, torture has been reduced, and intimidation and threats are no longer common. Contact with the outside world is allowed, and people are afforded the right to legal representation and defence. Yet, with a limited budget and little outside support, problems are mounting in Cambodian prisons. Lacking any working system of non-custodial control, the country faces rising crime and mounting prison populations. "The problem is that the increasing number of prisoners has not come with an increase in resources," prison authorities said. Cambodian prisons are sometimes forced to operate for months at a time without official provisions, relying entirely on humanitarian assistance and charity to feed the prisoners. NGO activists also worried about prison neglect. "Donors should be aware that transitional countries are faced with alternating increases of crime and attempts to assert the rule of law. This fills the prisons, which do not have the capacity to respond." AUSAID has recently provided help to develop and distribute a handbook of prison forms and procedures, along with training in its use and some complementary support for the physical improvement of five prison facilities. That support is welcome but, as Cambodian observers noted: "Today, many in the administration know the content of the standard minimum rules (for the treatment of prisoners), but do not have the resources or facilities to actually apply them."

South African beneficiaries suggested that the donor tendency to fund politically "safe" programmes can distort the democratic process and the accountability of public institutions. By way of example, the representative of a non-governmental organisation noted that donors sometimes fund NGOs and independent commissions to draft laws for the country, without regard for the role of parliament and the government. "Law drafting must be a job for those elected to do so, because they must be the ones held accountable by the people for the quality and success or failure of those laws. The job of NGOs and commissions is to comment and critique – but from a distance. Is honest critique by one of these independent bodies possible if they themselves are the drafter of the law?"

Beneficiaries in South Africa also observed that donors neglect prisons and prosecutors and opt for "safe courts and trendy police", as one said.[14] Prosecutors in South Africa wondered "why an institution so vital to fighting impunity is not viewed by most donors as an appropriate target of human rights assistance". Prisons, we were told by NGO staff, did little better. Prison authorities confirmed that prisons had received some human rights training support from local NGOs, as well as training and advisory services for revision of regulations from OHCHR, but virtually nothing beyond that. Advocates concerned by this situation explained how "most recently, [a major donor] drafted a two year plan of action for support to the sector, setting the categories of assistance that will be

---

[14] This observation was made both by prison authorities and advocates. What is "trendy" in most cases is human rights training for police. Support for police reform, as such, is much less so. (*Communication to the Council from DFID*, March 2000).

available during that time. The notable exclusion of prisons and penal reform means that organisations working in these areas will be unable to secure support from this donor during that time". Nor, added another, does this donor fund prisons directly, thus ruling out any hope for human rights assistance to the institution from that provider. A penal reform advocate summed up the situation by saying that "prisons and penal reform are not popular causes in most societies, and especially in transitional situations of high crime. Sufficient domestic support for this is therefore not available". An NGO activist agreed, noting that "women's rights, child rights, these are not controversial with donors. But prisoner rights are controversial with everyone".

In Guatemala, most donors felt that the human rights ombudsman and (some) NGOs were the only "safe" institutions before 1996 – though even here there was no consensus. Some donors abstained from supporting Guatemalan human rights NGOs for fear of offending the government, while others shied away from any official institution, including the ombudsman. In the period since 1996, the country seems to have settled into the same rather familiar pattern. Most donors have avoided prisons (although the UN is an important exception) and prosecutors, though to a lesser extent. (The *Ministerio Público* has received some UN, US and Canadian support.) Prosecutors said that the aid they have received is not enough to enable them to manage legal changes in the system and crime problems. Prison officials also face legal changes, new institutional demands, low public support, and critical transitional challenges, but must do so without significant assistance – for human rights or other needs. Prisoners, and penal reform, are low on the agenda in Guatemala, including the agenda of donors.

In Bulgaria, prosecutors have received almost no support, except in areas of work that relate to donor interests (like drugs and transnational crime). Prosecutors said they had not been consulted on the planning of legal reform, needs assessment, or project formulation. No new prison has been built in Bulgaria in over 60 years, and, said prison authorities, it shows. Conditions are poor and need is acute. In the absence of adequate non-custodial penal alternatives, prisons are over-used. Prison officials welcomed enthusiastically a recent offer from the Open Society Institute to provide training for prison officials and pilot treatment programmes, as well as a Bulgarian Helsinki Committee booklet on prisoner rights and a new pre-release programme (supported by Britain). Beyond these limited interventions, however, Bulgarian prison officials said that they had no reason to believe that prisons will soon become a reform priority.

Staying the course

Judging from the experience of the countries we have considered, it seems safe to say that reform is seldom a steady process. Official commitment to reform is rarely constant or continuous. Significant fluctuations are inevitable. Negotiating the ups and downs of reform processes, without reliable indicators by which to judge the political commitment to reform, is a difficult challenge for donors. It would certainly help if some reliable means were available to test the commitment to reform, and the extent of real progress in reforming the justice sector in line with international human rights standards. Some initial indicators emerge naturally from particular events, such as first time elections, peace agreements, popular revolutions, new constitutions, and major referenda. Once transitional processes have begun, however, subsequent indicators are more difficult to discern or assess objectively. It should be recognised that progress in the justice sector simply does not lend itself to short-term measurement of achievement. Donors who provide assistance to the justice sector can therefore expect a bumpy ride.

Beneficiaries seemed to urge above all that, despite the difficulties, donors should engage with official institutions and stay the course through the inevitable ups and downs. In other words, the commitment to reform must come from donors as well as official institutions in the country if justice sector reform is to progress. In our interviews, beneficiaries often wondered whether donors have the will to sustain support for justice reforms when it is inconvenient for them to do so — for example, because of their foreign policy interests, or domestic pressures to cut aid spending, or criticism by other governments. Here as in other aspects of the aid relationship, beneficiaries were looking for reciprocity. Both sides of the aid equation must be committed to staying the course for the (necessarily) long term.

Five: STRATEGIC REFORM

Considering that we looked at four different countries on four continents, the answers we heard were remarkably similar. The countries shared elements in common, of course. All were in transition during similar periods and most had been assisted by the same pool of donors. One central theme running through the responses was the need for a more strategic approach to justice sector development. A *strategic approach* combines many elements; we refer here mainly to the idea that aid to the justice sector should be seen as a whole, and positioned appropriately within broader development aid efforts; and to the need for clear planning, both of reforms and assistance efforts.

Opportunities to develop more strategic approaches to development emerged in 1998 and 1999 when, almost at the same time, the World Bank launched its Comprehensive Development Framework (CDF), the UN its Development Assistance Framework (UNDAF) and the High Commissioner for Human Rights a UN system-wide analysis of human rights-related assistance programmes. In parallel, more countries have begun to heed the recommendation of the World Conference on Human Rights (Vienna Declaration and Programme of Action) to adopt national plans of action in the field of human rights. Increasingly, these various initiatives are now being co-ordinated. Together, they promise more strategic, country-based approaches to human rights assistance in the justice sector. Nevertheless, each is still in its formative stages, none has yet proved its usefulness, and the degree to which they will complement or fit one another remains unclear. Thus far, little strategy, and even less effective co-ordination, have been evident on the ground.

Certainly strategic approaches to justice sector development have not been the rule in the four countries we studied. External support to the sector has largely been characterised by unconnected bilateral project agreements and *ad hoc* activities.[15] Clear national policy statements on the direction and objectives of reform have been mostly absent. Few comprehensive surveys have been undertaken to determine what has been done and what remains to be done. Much assistance has been provided without assessing needs thoroughly or consulting beneficiaries. Aid has not generally been guided by official national development planning for the sector. And co-ordination of programmes has been, in the words of one donor, "a complete disaster".

Beneficiaries told us that too often activities were implemented without advance research, without assessing needs, and without strategic planning. They said this was ineffective and wasted precious human and financial resources. "The biggest

---

[15] This is not to suggest beneficiaries are free of blame in this regard. Government officials in the recipient country, for example, may be anxious to "do something" during their time in office, an urge not easily satisfied by the commissioning of studies and plans, especially if implementation will take a decade or more.

need," said one academic in South Africa, "is for new strategies, based on honest needs assessment, common objectives, and open dialogue." Another beneficiary considered this so fundamental that aid which failed to respond to assessed needs should be rejected by the country.

Cambodian government officials, legal professionals, NGOs and activists (and also donors) agreed that development activities within the justice sector have been *ad hoc* and have not formed part of any carefully conceived plan, common vision, or agreed approach. All endorsed the view that a more strategic approach would be preferable, that much time had been lost, and that resources had been wasted as a result. One beneficiary spoke of "multiple donors, with various approaches, various models, and various plans". Others added that donors "had sub-contracted everything, even the thinking". The result, they said, was a fractured approach with "American, Japanese, Australian, French and other consultants each pushing their own models and agendas". Little effort and time has been spent on consulting local stakeholders. What was emerging as a result was "a piecemeal hodgepodge of a legal system, and a disempowered domestic constituency". Understandably, the call for a strategic and sector-wide approach had broad support among Cambodian beneficiaries.

Based upon our discussions with beneficiaries, we have identified four principal elements of a strategic approach for justice sector development. We discuss each in turn, below.

- Treating justice as a development sector, and seeing it as a whole
- Planning reforms and assistance activities properly
- Requiring participatory needs assessment
- Improving co-ordination.

Of course, no country can hope to demonstrate a perfect strategic approach, or to master all its elements. These are, nevertheless, key factors in more effective reform, and deserve donor support. In general, many of the shortcomings in aid that beneficiaries identified were due to a failure to invest up front in the substance and mechanisms of reform. Relatively little has been spent on careful research, effective methodology, and tailor made responses, and above all on investing at the start in building relationships and planning. While it has financial implications, a more strategic approach can help to remedy these recurrent shortcomings.

Recognising justice as a development sector
Development agencies customarily divide their activity into specific areas of focus (health, education, housing, etc.), often called "sectors" and "sub-sectors". Traditionally, "justice" has not been identified as a sector. Partly as a result, assistance to justice institutions is subject to confusion and duplication. Reforms are not conceived or implemented within a sufficiently comprehensive and

integrated framework. The crucial interrelationships between courts, prosecutors, defence lawyers, police, prison officials, etc., are insufficiently recognised. In all four of the countries studied, beneficiaries perceived the confusion of categories and concepts as a serious obstacle to effective assistance programmes. Donor budget lines reveal this confusion particularly clearly. Some list human rights as a category separate from justice, governance, civil society and health. Comments made by South African beneficiaries were similar to those raised in the other focus countries. An activist in Johannesburg noted that: "Donor categories make no sense. According to their categories, NGOs are not part of the justice sector, and human rights is something separate from development areas like poverty reduction, or health." We were told that this marginalises the concept of human rights, reducing it to "a sideline occupied by a small group of NGOs". They felt that development categories should be redesigned to create a new sector of justice alongside health, education, housing, and so on. Formulated in this way, human rights would cease to be a separate category and could be more appropriately integrated into development work in all its forms.

It was not only South African beneficiaries who believed that justice should be seen as a whole. Cambodian beneficiaries reported that donors speak of "human rights" to refer mainly to "NGOs" and do not associate human rights with economic, social or cultural rights. They said that "governance" is used with similar imprecision to describe anything in the official sector that does not fit other categories like "health" or "infrastructure". As a result it includes a hodgepodge of issues from anti-corruption measures to decentralisation, and from local administration to custodial abuse.

The experiences of beneficiaries in Guatemala were similar. We were told: "Neither donors nor local organisations have a shared vision of the boundaries between 'rule of law', 'human rights', 'democratisation', 'justice', and so on. There is a need to standardise the language here." Prosecutors agreed, one telling us that "the justice process is inter-linked, so support should be too, covering defence, prosecutions, courts, police, NGOs, and all other institutions".

Beneficiaries said that such fragmentation prevents the development of a strategic approach to the sector as a whole. In a democratic society, the administration of justice involves a diverse range of actors and institutions, which cuts across ministerial portfolios, branches of government and the official/non-governmental divide. Police, prisons, prosecutors, defence lawyers, judges, para-legals, NGOs, parliament, the ministries of justice and interior, and many other institutions all play a fundamental and interdependent role. Each is a stakeholder and each has a particular perspective and field of expertise to offer to the sector as a whole. All need to be involved in any genuine and effective process of reform.

It is therefore necessary to broaden and sharpen understanding of the language of development in these areas. Most important, justice should be understood as a development sector in its own right. One implication of such a re-ordering of categories might be that "human rights", rather than standing separately, would be integrated into development work in all areas.

NGOs as part of the justice sector

Non-governmental organisations are key actors in the justice sector in democratic countries, and are particularly important during periods of transition. Their role should be recognised in any reform efforts. One effect of failing to consider justice reform as a whole is to marginalise civil society. Certainly, donors fund NGOs to monitor the treatment of prisoners, criminal defendants and others, and to train police and prison guards. But the link is not made between those activities and justice sector reform as a whole. One donor told us that it had "not yet provided any support to the justice sector" though, in fact, this donor had made several grants to NGOs that monitored abuses in the system and trained justice officials. Several major donors confirmed that they treat support to NGOs and support to governments quite separately.

This issue relates directly to transparency and participation. NGOs and legal associations argue that the involvement of civil society in justice reform is essential and is an element of democratic development. Without full involvement, it was impossible for civil society groups to know the direction and pace of reforms, or whether reform proposals would respond to needs and shortcomings of the system that NGOs had identified. Beneficiaries argued that there is an important reservoir of expertise within non-governmental organisations that is useful to the justice sector. A number of Cambodian, Bulgarian, Guatemalan and South African NGOs have monitored and investigated abuses for some years and are familiar with many of the recurrent problems, needs and bottlenecks of the system, as well as with relevant national and international standards. In countries that lack skilled human resources, that knowledge and expertise is vital to effective planning and reform of the sector. Many in government recognise this, and those favouring reform usually see NGO participation as essential.

It should be emphasised again that, in the countries we visited, human rights NGOs agreed overwhelmingly that official institutions should receive human rights assistance, even when their human rights records are far from perfect. Their desire to be included in the sector, and to contribute their expertise to the reform process, cannot therefore be attributed to any wish to divert to themselves assistance received by official institutions.

Planning reform

Justice reform should be based on clear national policies and plans. Foreign support to those reforms should also be planned coherently, and donors have a role to play in developing national plans. Essentially, planning is about deciding what the intended goal is, what is required to achieve that goal, and apportioning tasks to different actors.

National policy

A clear national policy on justice sector reforms, setting out the official vision of the reform objectives, and committing the government to specific reforms necessary to realise that vision, is an important reference point for any strategic approach to justice development. The authority and broad parameters of such a policy may be rooted in the national constitution, the outcome of a referendum or other popular consultation, or even in the terms of peace agreements, but such instruments do not obviate the need for the policy statement itself. In most cases, this has been late in coming, or altogether absent.

While reforms have occurred in Cambodia, they have not done so as part of an integrated or planned process. The Constitution sets out the basic judicial structure, and references to justice institutions and objectives appear in official development documents, including commitments to reform, but one official confirmed that "we have no overall justice reform programme or national policy as such. There is nothing which links the various institutions of the justice system in a common approach and objective". Basic issues – such as whether the system should emphasise common law or civil law approaches – are as yet unresolved. No doubt blame lies with the government. But some beneficiaries believed that the uncoordinated and often competitive approach of donors is at least partly responsible. They described situations in which several donors lobbied the government to adopt positions that matched their different priorities. One emphasised economic and investment aspects, another civil law approaches to criminal justice, another the common law model, another judicial responses to selected groups such as children, etc. Beneficiaries argued that Cambodia needed a clear statement of public policy, describing the nature and direction of the justice system, and that such a policy should be developed in a public and participatory fashion.

Guatemala, on the other hand, has a clear, public and detailed statement of its reform policy in the form of the peace agreements. Foreign Ministry officials told us that "the peace accords are the official reference point for justice reforms, setting specific commitments, objectives, and time-frames". The agreements are indeed detailed, and wide-ranging. They contain specific commitments on a host of issues, among them human rights, indigenous peoples, a (truth) commission on historical clarification, socio-economic and agrarian reforms, civil power and democratisation, and constitutional reform. This, we were told, provided a welcome and essential direction to the reform efforts, even if those efforts have so far not advanced to the satisfaction of most.

Specific plans for the justice sector

In addition to the need for a policy commitment to reform, beneficiaries in all the countries we visited stated that detailed plans for the justice sector were also essential. Many considered such plans provided the best foundations for donor support and co-ordination, as well as for setting benchmarks and measuring progress. The process has evolved differently in each country but none, according to beneficiaries, could claim complete success. Each nevertheless offered lessons about the process of planning justice sector reforms and its importance.

Bulgarians told us that no real plan for justice sector reforms existed in that country in 1999. Government officials referred to the country's plan for European integration (Agenda 2001 and the National Programme of Action for the *Acquis*). None of them suggested, however, that these documents contain a detailed strategic plan for the sector. The reason, NGOs and officials said, is that there was no real reform process prior to 1997. Previous governments issued statements about reforms but had "no commitment, and no programme". In this context, aid to the sector had been entirely by way of unconnected *ad hoc* donor projects. By mid-1999, a process had finally been launched, with technical support from the Council of Europe (Centre for the Study of Democracy) and funding from other donors. Beneficiaries hoped that the so-called *Judicial Reform Initiative* would form the basis for a comprehensive development plan.

With support from donors, South Africa has produced several impressive planning documents, including a national plan of action for human rights, a justice sector development plan called *Justice Vision 2000*, and a *White Paper on Safety and Security* detailing a medium term approach to improving public safety. Collectively, these cover the full range of justice sector institutions and challenges. South African observers said that they were detailed, specific and strategic in conception.

The problem, said both NGO and official beneficiaries, is not with the documents but the process of implementation. For example, the three documents are not linked to form parts of a strategic whole. The principal justice sector plan (*Justice Vision 2000*) is generally agreed to be very good, but officials in the sector admitted that many in the sector are unaware of it, and others do not see its relevance to their work. "It is a very good plan," said one observer, "but it was prepared in a donor process with donor funds by a small group of South African academics outside the justice system. It was not linked directly to the budget of the Justice Department, nor to the work of the people employed in the sector, who in any event didn't participate in its development, and thus do not feel committed to it." [16] Most of the officials we met believed the initiative was important and might create conditions for a more strategic and efficient development of the sector. But to realise that potential, its implementation needs sustained support, involving all stakeholders in the sector. In particular, a continuation of the consultation process launched during the drafting of the plan[17] could do much to dispel the perception by some that the plan is "external", and to encourage a greater sense of ownership.

South Africa also has a *National Plan of Action for Human Rights* which was prepared in a broadly participatory way. A broad range of NGOs and government institutions were involved in its development, revision and adoption. South African proponents of the plan see it as a valuable tool that empowers NGOs, independent commissions and advocates of reform, by establishing express and measurable benchmarks of progress against which to hold the government accountable. Others recognise the quality of the plan's content and its potential as a reform tool, but think it was too much an "event", rather than a process: reviving the plan's follow-up process, NGO representatives told us, was crucial.

In addition to lacking a clear national policy on reform, Cambodia has no specific reform plan for the justice sector. Ministry of Justice officials confirmed that nothing is in place to ensure that interventions are efficiently implemented and integrated. Others observed that efficient progress could not be made without a system-wide, planned approach, based on assessed needs, and with some oversight mechanism. While the absence of a reform plan for the sector has clearly contributed to the rather chaotic and *ad hoc* nature of assistance thus far, Cambodia will soon have a new opportunity to benefit from a structured planning process. Officials told us that the World Bank will be preparing a country assistance strategy for Cambodia. At the same time, Cambodia has been designated by the United Nations as a so-called "UNDAF country", meaning that UN agencies will work with the country's institutions to develop a more co-ordinated development framework. Donors involved in human rights assistance to the sector are also engaged in, or planning to start, reviews of their work that offer new opportunities for planning initiatives. We were told that the next phase of human rights assistance and reform could be far more effective if a plan were developed (and supported by donors).

In Guatemala, one beneficiary told us that "we have many plans – all of them imaginative and imaginary". His concern, and that of many we spoke to, was that, in spite of much planning, implementation seems to advance slowly. It is true that Guatemala has many plans for the sector, including the reform parameters of the peace accords, the detailed and strategic project documents of the World Bank,

---

[16] Advisers involved in the project to develop the plan explained that the Minister of Justice chose to work with a team of South African specialists outside the Ministry partly to circumvent "old guard" officials not committed to transformation and reform, and partly to inject fresh ideas and progressive thinking. (*Communication to the Council from the Danish Centre for Human Rights*, 1 March 2000.)

[17] The difference between the perception by some stakeholders that they were not involved, and claims by the Planning Unit charged with drafting the plan that stakeholders were broadly consulted cannot be explained based upon the limited discussion that we had in the country. The Danish Centre for Human Rights, which served as a consultant for Danida on the project ("Transformation of the Justice Sector in South Africa") reported that some 3000 people were consulted during the drafting phase. (*Communication to the Council from the Danish Centre for Human Rights*, 1 March 2000.)

MINUGUA, UNDP, Inter-Development Bank (IDB), USAID, and the EU. There is also a Plan for the Modernisation of the Judiciary 1997-2002 (*Plan de Modernizacion del Organismo Judicial 1997-2002*), developed by the Judiciary Modernisation Commission (*Comisión de Modernizacion del Organismo Judicial*) and adopted by the Supreme Court which appointed it. A government-appointed Judicial Sector Strengthening Commission (*Comisión de Fortalecimiento de la Justicia*), established pursuant to the peace accords (*Fortalecimiento del Poder Civil y Función del Ejercito en una Sociedad Democratica*), prepared a broader justice sector plan and issued a report covering plans for the entire sector, including lawyers, prosecutors, courts, law schools and others. A justice sector co-ordination body, the *Instancia Coordinadora de la Modernizacion del Sector Justicia*, which was formed by the Supreme Court, the *Ministerio Público* (including prosecutors), the *Ministerio de Gobernacion* (including police and prisons) and the national Public Defender Institute (*Instituto de la Defensa Pública Penal*), has prepared a Strategic Sectoral Plan (*Plan Estratégico Sectorial*), which was undergoing important revisions in the summer of 1999. The *Ministerio de Gobernacion* (Ministry of Interior) has now developed its own strategic plan, including a sub-plan for the penitentiary system. Finally, Guatemala is developing a national plan of action for human rights, which will itself address aspects of this sector.

While this makes for a rather complex mix of plans and committees, there is no doubt that Guatemala (and foreign donors there) have attached importance to justice sector reform and planning. Guatemalans involved in the process offered some valuable advice on the basis of their experience. They suggested that donor support for the reform process was crucial and gave particular credit to UNDP here. They said that official support is equally important to successful implementation (and has been problematic in Guatemala). Additionally, they suggested that care should be taken to link plans, wherever planning occurs at several levels. Finally, they said that broad participation and public information are important, to create institutional and public support.

Tracking reform
Most beneficiaries in our focus countries argued that no readily available, comprehensive source of data and information on progress in justice sector reforms was available. In particular, little information was available to show what projects were underway and which donors were providing assistance. Those concerned with reform in government, NGOs or donor agencies, therefore, waste much time searching for basic information. Resources are also wasted, because activities are duplicated. One suggestion to overcome these problems is that prior to commencing a co-ordinated reform programme for the sector, and periodically thereafter, a survey should be undertaken to determine what has been done, what has been planned for the immediate term, and what remains to be addressed.

In Guatemala, a UNDP supported survey has been undertaken and maintained (a job which, staff pointed out, is complicated by the failure of some donors to co-operate). The result is a "justice sector matrix" – a snapshot of the status of the justice sector reform which makes planning on "next steps" much easier. Originally focused on official institutions and activities, the survey is now being expanded to include civil society actors. Other donors (including the World Bank) appear to have undertaken similar exercises, albeit largely in parallel and in connection with the development of their own projects.

In Cambodia, Bulgaria and South Africa, on the other hand, no such exercise had been undertaken recently, and beneficiaries thought a review of activities and developments was overdue. Many donors now provide forms of human rights assistance and many initiatives are planned or have started. Beneficiaries described several separate training programmes, legislative drafting exercises, and advisory arrangements running in parallel in the three countries. While some donors may have surveyed the sector in connection with their own activities before launching programmes, no such survey was available, except in Guatemala, during our visits. Beneficiaries agreed that such a survey would usefully map what has already been accomplished, what is "in the pipeline", and what needs to be started.

Participatory needs assessment

Beneficiaries in all four countries told us that donors failed to assess needs in a thorough and consultative way. They considered this was one of the most serious and most common flaws of human rights assistance to the justice sector. An initial assessment of needs, capacities, priorities, risks and options was widely seen as indispensable. Some donors, we heard, simply drafted projects at headquarters and appeared with ready-made and inevitably inappropriate and even unworkable packages. Others fielded missions ostensibly for needs assessment, then delivered projects which did not reflect beneficiary advice or actual needs.

Most Bulgarian beneficiaries observed that consultative needs assessment was almost entirely absent in human rights assistance to the country. They said that some providers conducted no assessment at all and simply "entered with a pre-conceived agenda, which they then package in project bureaucracy". Others, we were told, "went through the motions of needs assessment" but in the end produced projects that did not take local advice into account. An assessment of needs across the justice sector was due to be undertaken by the EU at the end of 1999, according to officials.

Cambodian beneficiaries also said that very little needs assessment had been done in the justice sector. "Foreigners too often fly in with preconceived, general packages rather than finding out first what the real needs are," said one official. Indeed, most of the beneficiaries with whom we spoke in Cambodia said that they had rarely been consulted as part of a needs assessment process. Beneficiaries also pointed out that assessments rarely took place before training was done. One prosecutor, after noting the highly general content of courses, politely suggested that "training itself might be more carefully targeted through assessments". To this, nevertheless, there were encouraging exceptions. We were made aware of at least two needs assessments conducted in the sector, by AUSAID in 1994 and by the Canadian International Development Agency (CIDA) in 1999. AUSAID representatives advised that it was vital to "involve all local stakeholders from the start, to avoid snags and resistance later". Beneficiaries agreed, and added that the lack of a consultative needs assessment could effectively render a project illegitimate. One NGO employee said: "Donors must stop this flavour of the month club. All [assistance] must be based on local realities as determined through a consultative needs assessment."

Beneficiaries in South Africa, where there is much expertise in human rights law and justice administration, raised the problem repeatedly. The "parachute approach" of donors was said to be both insulting and wasteful, although some of the beneficiaries we interviewed indicated that at least some donors did try genuinely to consult. Where this was the case, beneficiaries found the resulting programmes to be far more credible than those formulated without adequate consultation.[18]

Guatemalan beneficiaries identified a tendency to assess needs through "ceremonial contact" at higher (usually ministry) levels, without sufficient consultation with working-level justice institutions, NGOs, or communities (especially Mayan). Some official institutions described how projects and consultants "suddenly appeared" without notice, owing to a failure of aid providers to consult directly with beneficiary institutions. One official recalled that she was surprised when a foreign technical expert arrived at her institution one day, with written terms of reference, pre-established objectives, and an assignment to work in the institution as part of a donor project. The two governments had agreed based on donor assumptions "about what was good for us". Beneficiaries in the country repeatedly emphasised that there is no reasonable alternative to careful, consultative needs assessment. A judge told us that: "Donors must link directly with the beneficiary institutions, assess needs, listen to concerns, see existing capacities, hear our priorities, and only then offer their support."

---

[18] The EU Foundation is one successful example, and seems to have avoided many of the problems and criticisms of the EU in other countries. We were told the Foundation assessed needs for its programmes through an 18 month process of dialogue and negotiations with partners, including both NGOs and government offices.
(*Communication to the Council from Nicolas Marcoux*, Director, EU Foundation for Human Rights in South Africa, 28 February 2000.)

Improving co-ordination

It would seem self-evident that strategic development of the justice sector requires systematic and meaningful co-ordination, between donors and with the various national institutions and actors involved in the reform process. While beneficiaries and donors alike agreed on its importance, co-ordination has not usually been successful. There appears to be a commitment in principle among donors to co-ordinate their assistance activities, but in practice it rarely seems to materialise. In many cases, each donor's need to ensure the visibility of its own projects hampers effective co-ordination.

At the national level, co-ordination has been difficult due to the variety of actors involved, including representatives of all three branches of government, NGOs, professional organisations and independent commissions. Government beneficiaries, NGO beneficiaries and donors in most of the countries studied (Guatemala was the exception – and here as well it was far from perfect) all agreed that there was essentially no co-ordination of programmes or activities in the sector, either among donors or more broadly among beneficiaries, and that problems of waste, duplication and reduced transparency were the result. All agreed that some form of justice/rule of law co-ordination group should be established (with the exception of one donor representative, who indicated that he did not believe in donor co-ordination structures, because "they only invited argument").

Bulgaria is a telling example, although signs of improved co-ordination appeared recently. For most of the decade, co-ordination of aid in the sector was almost entirely lacking. Bulgaria now has two emerging co-ordination structures for the sector: the *Judicial Reform Initiative*, and the *Judicial Development and Court Administration Programme* (also known as the *Magistrates School Programme*). These, beneficiaries said, were developed in parallel and will need to be linked. Each has separate donors, separate project counterparts, and separate implementation structures. By mid-1999, however, donors and beneficiaries in the sector had at least begun to discuss how they could address these problems.

Nor does the Cambodian experience offer a model for co-ordination. At a consultative group meeting of donors providing aid to Cambodia in Tokyo in June 1999, a proposal to establish a co-ordination sub-group on the rule of law in Cambodia was "allowed to fizzle out" according to one participant. Other participants confirmed that quarterly co-ordination meetings with standing groups were agreed for public administration, forests, demobilisation, fiscal and financial reform, and the social sector. But, because donors did not support the idea and participants were not willing to lobby for it, no quarterly group was formed to deal with the justice sector. One beneficiary suspected that donors stood back, assuming this matter was "sensitive and political", even though it was generally agreed that such a mechanism would be useful. Among UN agencies, the Office of the High Commissioner for Human Rights convenes a "governance theme group" but, apart from UNDP and OHCHR itself, none of the major donors to the sector are UN agencies and thus do not participate. Nor apparently has Cambodia's central development planning and co-ordination process, the Council for the Development of Cambodia (CDC) and its National Programme, enhanced effective co-ordination within the justice sector. According to officials in the sector, "the CDC co-ordination process has not worked for the justice sector, facilitating neither support nor co-ordination. During five years of use of the CDC process, no assistance was received, and less than 0.05% of the budget went to justice". This would seem to be consistent with the tendency of officials in the sector to now deal directly with potential donors. As for the government's proposal to form a national council on judicial reform, we were told that, as of July 1999, this was the only one of several reform bodies proposed by the government that had not been established.

Beneficiaries and also donors in South Africa agree that co-ordination in the sector has been lacking there as well. One exception was an initiative by the South African Police Services (SAPS) to ensure co-ordinated use of human rights assistance. The SAPS established an internal human rights unit and appointed two full-time, specialist officers to run it. The programme generated an impressive series of human rights training tools and materials, and a string of pilot activities which, according to officials, "took the best from what all the various donors had to offer, and then created a distinctly South African programme". Throughout the process, control was exercised by the human rights unit, forcing donors to participate in a complementary way and on the beneficiary's terms. However, this appeared to be an exceptional experience. Local NGOs told us that donor competition, rather than co-ordination, was the norm. They said some donors used domestic organisations to compete against each other. Donors agreed that co-ordination has been lacking. Some said the government had not been able to co-ordinate the sector. Others pointed out that some donors oppose co-ordination; limited co-ordination within the EU, for example, had not been extended to non-EU donors. The result, according to NGOs we met, was duplication of activities and gaps in the assistance offered to the justice sector.

While not boasting perfect co-ordination, Guatemala differs markedly in this regard as it does in matters of planning. Formal co-ordination of Guatemala's justice sector takes place at several levels: between UN agencies (it is hoped the UNDAF process, under way in Guatemala, will further enhance this); between donors and UN agencies in a UNDP co-ordinated process with a detailed matrix of activities and monthly co-ordination meetings; between judicial officials within the *Comisión de Modernizacion del Organismo Judicial*; and between all major institutions of the sector within the *Instancia Coordinadora de la Modernizacion del Sector Justicia*. As with planning, Guatemala has thus taken co-ordination of justice sector development seriously. This does not mean that co-ordination has been unproblematic. On the contrary, said beneficiaries. The *Instancia*, which is the central co-ordinating body for justice reforms, was only officially mandated in November of 1998, two years into the process. It has lacked funds, equipment, technical staff and sufficient office facilities. The *Instancia's* highly respected Executive Secretary is also a sitting judge of the Supreme Court and chair of the Judicial Modernisation Commission. While this has obvious benefits in terms of the body's credibility and capacity, some said that a single official cannot indefinitely manage the workload. The *Instancia* has no permanent technical secretariat.

Additionally, beneficiaries working with the body say that some donors have continued to ignore the co-ordination offered by the *Instancia*, "chasing their own priorities and projects without bothering to plug in to the process," according to one Guatemalan official. This is all the more problematic because many donors are funding numerous projects in the sector. By 1999, the list of donors with significant involvement in the justice sector included MINUGUA, UNDP, the International Bank for Reconstruction and Development (IBRD), IDB, EU, USAID, Spain, Denmark, the Netherlands, Canada, Sweden and Norway. Beneficiaries said that failure to co-ordinate has resulted in duplication of activity and unhelpful competition between donors over national models for police, courts and codes. Some bilateral donors have opted to contribute through the UN (MINUGUA and UNDP) in order "to avoid complicating the mix". Clearly, donor co-ordination, in Guatemala as elsewhere, depends on donor commitment.

The assumption that donors, rather than the recipient governments, should be responsible for co-ordination is increasingly rejected by donors and beneficiaries alike. At the same time, there is growing recognition that national governments need technical and financial support to enable them to co-ordinate well. Finally, as it is recognised that participation is essential, national NGOs will need to be involved in co-ordination as in other aspects of the reform process. Sector co-ordination that is led by the host government, involves NGOs, and is based upon a common strategy and the instruments described in this section (policy, survey, plan, etc.), may have a better hope of succeeding.

Five strategic safeguards
In this chapter, we have emphasised that a *strategic* approach to justice sector reform requires numerous elements. The justice sector must be seen as a whole, the reform process and foreign assistance need to be planned and co-ordinated, and assistance should be based on a clear understanding of local needs and capacities. Of course, such elements may be seen as essential to any area of development assistance. Certain aspects of justice sector reforms nevertheless require particular attention in planning and implementation – for the most part to ensure that those who are most disadvantaged under the existing institutions benefit from their reform. Based upon our discussions with beneficiaries, we have

identified five safeguards to address this need.

- Ensure access to justice and institutions of redress;
- Recognise indigenous systems;
- Empower women;
- Involve minorities directly;
- Make the link between human rights and personal security.

Access to justice

Development of new institutions, or reform and strengthening of old ones, will have value only to the extent that those institutions are accessible, especially to the poor and those who are excluded from society. Every strategy for reform of the justice sector should give attention to issues of access. Of course, even in advanced democracies it is difficult to ensure that all sectors of society have access to justice. But developing countries, and those in transition, face exceptional problems. For some countries, systems are so underdeveloped that access to lawyers, courts, alternative dispute resolution, human rights bodies, or other avenues of redress is difficult for everyone. In others, institutions function but barriers of class, race, gender, language, religion and geography prevent some groups and individuals who are most subject to discrimination or exclusion from using them. Accessibility therefore involves far more than the physical creation of new institutions or offices. It is equally necessary to make institutions economically, socially, linguistically and culturally accessible. If attention is not given to issues of access, assistance for reform may merely reinforce the privileges of those who are already advantaged.

Each of the countries we visited has developed particular approaches to the question of access. Guatemala has "justice centres", Cambodia and South Africa a network of paralegals (called "defenders" in Cambodia), and Bulgarian lawyers use strategic litigation before the European Court of Human Rights on behalf of large, excluded sectors of society. Human rights assistance has been channelled to support each of these initiatives to varying degrees and, according to beneficiaries, with some success.

Access to justice in Cambodia suffers from all of the usual barriers of under-resourced and under-developed justice systems in countries across the globe. Cambodians face certain additional challenges, however, because of their unique history. Few lawyers survived the Khmer Rouge terror. Even today, there are only between 150 and 220 lawyers in the country (domestic counts vary).[19] They are supplemented by trained "defenders" and the NGO Legal Aid of Cambodia (LAC).

---

[19] Koy Neam of The Asia Foundation puts the number at 216, citing licensing numbers of the Bar Association of the Kingdom of Cambodia. He notes that several of the non-lawyer "defenders" were accredited by the Bar Association after 1997 and are now recognised as lawyers. (*Communication to the Council*, March 2000.)

For most Cambodians, however, official justice is not an option. LAC does not have the resources to finance the very large number of Cambodians who would qualify for legal aid. External support for para-legal "defenders" has dwindled in recent years.

Inequality in South Africa is evident in relation to justice. Beneficiaries told us that donors, satisfied that the new constitutional dispensation and its institutions have buried the *apartheid* past, were "too quick to celebrate". As elsewhere on the continent, poor, rural, black communities have little or no access to legal advice. The growth of capable NGOs, the transformation of the justice system, the reform of legal aid, and the country's expanding pool of qualified para-legals, offered the promise of enhanced access. By mid-1999, nonetheless, the situation had worsened rather than improved. Paralegals and NGOs faced a funding crisis triggered by the departure of some donors (post-*apartheid*) and the decision of others to shift their funding from civil society to government. The official Legal Aid Board collapsed, bankrupted by inefficient management and abuses by participating lawyers. In the new institutions of justice, several beneficiaries told us that those that have benefited most have been persons from the historically privileged groups of South Africa. Most poor and black citizens remain without effective access. Legal aid is expected to be revamped, and South Africa is experimenting with new access mechanisms, such as a more co-ordinated and professional paralegal corps. A pilot justice centre has been established in the Western Cape, as a co-operative initiative between the government, the Legal Aid Board, the National Community Based Paralegal Association and Lawyers for Human Rights. It aims to develop a model for reform of the national legal aid programme. According to South African jurists and activists nevertheless, at the end of 1999 South Africa had an impressive new justice system – but only for some.

Guatemala's donor-supported plans and its efforts to enhance access to justice have taken many forms. These include increasing the number of justices of the peace, expanding the judicial infrastructure, introducing alternative dispute mechanisms, "integrating" indigenous dispute resolution, and piloting "justice centres" in outlying and rural areas. Justice centres have been one of the most popular experiments. They have been supported by MINUGUA (which originated the model), UNDP, USAID, the IDB, the World Bank and others. The essential idea is to post permanent, integrated, justice system satellites in rural areas to provide access to otherwise excluded (mostly indigenous) populations. The model has been praised, rightly, as creative and practical. However, donors, officials and NGOs do not consider it is a perfect success. In many cases, the centres did not achieve integration. Though many Mayans speak no Spanish, the centres had inadequate translation facilities. Other observers noted that not enough was done to win the trust of local communities, which for decades had been terrorised by official institutions. Nor were the centres linked to pre-existing Mayan legal processes. Many Guatemalans involved with the centres, however, see merit in the idea and are pleased that, rather than abandoning the initiative, donors and the government have engaged in a series of "lessons learned" processes and are now working to correct flaws in the model.

Access to judicial remedies is beyond the reach of most Bulgarians, according to human rights advocates and lawyers in the country. Public confidence in the legal system (including courts and prosecutors) is lower than for any other state institution. Reform of the justice sector was only beginning in 1999, and effective access could not be anticipated in the short or medium terms. Lawyers and NGOs have therefore adopted alternative strategies, including use of the European Court on Human Rights, to establish precedents and secure justice for large classes of disadvantaged people. The government's strong wish to achieve EU membership has made it highly responsive to the Court's rulings, and Bulgarian lawyers have claimed several successes. At the same time, an ongoing debate in the country has aligned proponents of an ombudsman institution against advocates of a national human rights commission, as alternative vehicles for increased access. As yet it is unclear what effect the addition of one (or two) more institution will have on the support donors offer. Will access to the justice system be improved, or will under-funded alternative institutions, just like the courts, be inaccessible to those who need them most?

Recognise indigenous systems

Experience in countries with significant indigenous communities suggests that attempts to improve their access to the justice sector will fail if they are not fully involved in related planning and decision-making and if pre-existing indigenous legal systems and traditions are not recognised. However, that lesson, while clear, is far from simple to act upon. Many donors and their national partners struggle to balance competing human rights interests in countries that have indigenous traditions. Summing up the perceived tension, the Guatemalan Truth Commission report recommended that: "what is known as customary law is recognised and integrated into the Guatemalan legal framework [...] *as long as the rights recognised in the Guatemalan Constitution and international treaties on human rights are not violated.*" [Emphasis added.][20]

Efforts at integration do not meet with approval from all indigenous groups. Some indigenous advocates in Guatemala wondered why it is necessary to discuss so frequently "integration" of Mayan customary legal systems in the national legal system. "If Mayans are not part of the economic and social system of the country, why should they be forced to be part of the legal system?" asked one. The word "integration" is controversial in many of these discussions, and some Mayan representatives prefer "recognition and co-ordination" instead. According to one:

[20] *Guatemala: Memory of Silence* (TZ'INIL NA'TAB'AL), Report of the Commission for Historical Clarification (CEH, Guatemala, 1999).

"The issue should be legal co-ordination, of two parallel systems, not integration. If you integrate it, it ceases to be Mayan law and will disappear, along with the largest vehicle in the country for conflict resolution and justice access." Others agreed, saying "if you integrate it, you must write it. If you write it you make it precedent-driven and static. At this point, it ceases to be indigenous law".

Indigenous representatives also believed that lack of direct contact between donors and indigenous groups created "misunderstandings". "We have often heard donors refer to the idea that Mayan systems allow for cruel forms of punishment. This is a misconception. We see international standards as consistent with our own. Mayan law has nothing to do with cruel sanctions. It focuses on reparations, conflict resolution and practical community based solutions." Sanctions, we were told, are essentially about compensation and bringing a return to equilibrium. Others agreed, saying that it is often ignorance of indigenous law that leads to false perceptions. "Lynching, for example, which has appeared in some communities, is not a Mayan legal phenomenon (as some claim), but simply an emotional, fear-based response as in other communities." Indigenous representatives also noted that customary law applies by consensus and consent and anyone can opt out and choose the national legal system, if they wish.

All states have an obligation to provide a legal system that protects human rights in a manner consistent with international standards, and that is accessible to all persons present within its borders. Equally clearly, at least as regards the bringing of civil claims, individuals must be free to decide whether to seek to access that system or not. In Guatemala, however, the debate has not been an easy one, and indigenous communities are not at all satisfied that their voice has been heard in efforts to resolve it. What is more, while most human rights advocates support indigenous demands for two separate systems (national and indigenous), some believe the outcome is a "separate and unequal" one, in which the privileged minority would enjoy a well-financed and ultimately effective legal system while the poor majority would have to make do with a poor system. In the end, most of those involved in this debate agreed on at least two points: first, indigenous communities must be fully involved in development planning that purports to address their justice needs; and second, the indigenous system must be formally recognised in law.

Empower women

Special attention should be given to ensuring that reform of the justice sector addresses the needs and status of women. Too often such attention is largely superficial, amounting to adding gender references to project documents, or holding a few workshops on women's rights. Rarely have empowerment strategies featured in these approaches. Many of those to whom we spoke raised these issues in the countries we visited.

Levels of domestic violence, rape and trafficking are all high in Cambodia. Women's advocates and human rights organisations in Cambodia believe that donors are sensitive to the abuse of Cambodian women and have supported their work. Several beneficiaries in Phnom Penh said that "All donors will support projects or organisations with 'women' in the title". Yet they also said they believed that donors too often take a superficial "checklist approach" to gender and women's issues and fail to maximise potential impact. One Khmer women's activist insisted that "especially in matters relating to gender and women, donors must discard the checklists and look at the real situation on the ground".

In some cases donors have made important contributions. Their support has enabled impressive local NGOs to begin to counter the enormous threats confronting women.[21] This has been vital, and women believed it should be continued and expanded. Nevertheless, "donors should discard their checklists and opt instead for dialogue, communication, and partnership, and a focus on the specific realities of Cambodian women". Assessing needs on the ground, through direct consultations and sustained relationships with local partners was the better approach. Beneficiaries said that training courses and workshops about gender, often supported by donors, are not enough. An activist explained that: "trafficking is not a product of ignorance of human rights standards, but a product of poverty, with families selling their daughters to survive". Advancing the position of women means addressing the root causes of their situation. Assistance earmarked for women's advancement should also therefore be directed to creative local projects for increasing economic and social options. Additionally, beneficiaries pointed out that strengthening the justice system itself helped to protect women. Many believed that far too little had been done in this regard. The few shelters available were not adequate. At present, we were told, the justice system offers virtually no protection for women victims. Courts are difficult to access. While the law on assault can be applied, no specific law on domestic violence has been passed.

In South Africa too, the protection of women's rights is of great concern. It is estimated that two million rapes occur each year in the country. Here too, we were told that while donors support women's rights projects, they do not respond adequately to real needs. NGOs told us that it is reasonably easy to find donor support for "standard gender projects", like workshops or promotional activities, but not for strategies "that don't fit neatly into simplistic donor approaches". For example, no major donors agreed to fund NGOs who wanted to strengthen prosecutions through a "gender in criminal justice" project. In the end, say organisers, the initiative was funded by a private foundation.

---

[21] Among them the Women's Media Centre of Cambodia (which uses the media to produce radio and TV programmes to advance the status of Cambodian women); the Cambodian Women's Crisis Centre (working with women in crisis, providing women's shelters and centres), and Women for Prosperity (focused on women in leadership, women and the law, and empowerment strategies).

The social context in Guatemala is characterised by intersecting forces of racism, urban bias, and gross disparities of wealth and power – the latter with regard both to women and to indigenous peoples, and thus Mayan women are doubly disadvantaged. Superficial approaches to gender in Guatemala have done little to convince beneficiaries that all donors are committed to women's rights. Indigenous activists say that "some donors simply fund their western priorities, such as women's rights, while avoiding issues like racism and Mayan empowerment. If an NGO puts the word "women" in the title of a project, regardless of its merit it will be funded, perhaps drawing funds away from a more urgent project on indigenous problems. In the end, this would hurt indigenous women – who are already doubly-marginalised and doubly-victimised". Representatives of a women's organisation thought some donors "deal with women and gender in a cosmetic fashion, which is satisfied with workshops held by elite organisations. Support for empowerment, on the other hand, is much less available". Guatemalan beneficiaries appealed for a more careful approach to this sensitive issue, based not on donor formulae but realities on the ground. An activist observed that "taking the easy way out for donors usually means supporting projects of strong, Guatemala City-based NGOs. But in a country where there is still little solidarity between Mayan and non-Mayan women, funding rich and élite groups does little to help those representing powerless, rural, poor, indigenous women". Others said that donors needed to learn how to recognise the sensitive social and cultural implications of these issues and avoid approaches that seek "just to teach the latest buzz words to local women". "The 'how' of women's advancement in a particular society has to be determined by partners from that society, not by a donor manual." The better approach, we were told, was based on a much clearer understanding of local realities.

Involve minorities directly

Minorities have not fared much better, according to those we interviewed. In Bulgaria, where minority Roma, Turks and Muslims face particular discrimination and high levels of poverty, members of these communities and their advocates say they rarely benefit from human rights assistance. Most of the support they receive appears to come from Bulgarian and Eastern European human rights organisations, whose members are sensitive to the problems of these communities. Direct support from external donors is said to be extremely limited and rare. Minority organisations often carry out human rights activities on a shoe-string budget and on a largely voluntary basis. They provide legal assistance and have engaged in anti-discrimination advocacy (including a class action suit against public utilities that discriminated against minority communities). To whom do they turn for support for these activities? "Local human rights groups are our biggest supporters," said one minority representative. "We have very little contact with donors, who prefer to work on minority issues through the majority organisations in Sophia." A Roma activist explained that "most donor money is spent on funding non-Roma organisations to study the Roma. Almost nothing comes to us directly". The result, minority beneficiaries told us, is lost opportunities for donors to contribute to empowerment and capacity building in minority communities. "For ten years, donors did not allow us to take responsibility for our own human rights projects, preferring to channel assistance through the [non-minority] organisations in Sophia. Ten years ago, neither they nor we had capacity. Today, as a result, they do, but we still do not. And what happens now? Donors implement through the other organisations because they have better capacity."

Nor, say Cambodian beneficiaries, do Vietnamese or the minority Cham receive much attention or support from donors. Minority organisations and their advocates in Cambodia point out that organisations promoting minority rights in Cambodian society simply could not survive without external donor support. They do survive largely through support from the UN (OHCHR) and some Khmer NGOs, for which they are quick to express gratitude. Other donors, they said, had declined to help. One minority representative commented: "We are among the most poor, and the most vulnerable, and the last to benefit from domestic institutions. Donors should help directly. What message do they send if even human rights assistance is discriminatory?"

Make the link between human rights and personal security
Transitional periods are typically marked by high levels of insecurity brought on by economic crisis, rising crime rates, and limited law enforcement capacity. Rising levels of violent crime and corresponding fear among the public can create sharp policy issues for governments in transition. Beneficiaries said that, as popular demand grew for police, prosecutors, and more prisons to cope with crime, tolerance of "tough" policing and eventually for official abuse increases too. Human rights advocates, yesterday's heroes, suddenly become "friends of criminals", and public support for human rights wanes. Various approaches to human rights assistance can combat or reinforce this public perception. Many donors, beneficiaries pointed out, have one budget line for human rights and another for law enforcement. Properly conceived, human rights and law enforcement are intertwined, since an effective police force not only respects the rights of those it apprehends but also takes positive measures to protect ordinary citizens. If donors treat law enforcement as separate from human rights, they may reinforce trends that undermine support for the rule of law, and confuse public opinion about human rights.

Even before the effective implementation of new human rights guarantees, Guatemalan NGOs and officials told us that they are faced by the "human rights versus security" issue. Rising fear of crime, together with an ineffective justice system, have led to huge court backlogs, and lynching had begun in rural areas. "In this situation," one activist said, "we [human rights advocates] are seen as defenders of the criminals and enemies of law and order". Similarly, for Bulgarians, the decade of transition has brought dramatically increased crime rates; they more than tripled between 1989 and 1992, and rose to frightening levels during the socio-economic crisis of 1996-97. As a result, we were told, people in Bulgaria feel extremely insecure. Activists pointed out that this, combined with popular racist notions that certain minorities are more criminal, has made it much harder to advance human rights ideas.

South African human rights workers and justice officials share a similar experience. They said that they have watched the pendulum swing from "security and repression" under *apartheid* to "human rights" under the new constitutional and political order, and then back to "security" as violent crime has risen in the country. In this atmosphere, human rights officials and activists warned, donors and beneficiaries must take special care to re-link the concepts of human rights and security in project activities. "This situation is very dangerous," said one, "because people don't realise that the police of today are largely still the police of the *apartheid* era. Encouraging them to push the rules in fighting crime could easily backfire on the very communities calling for that approach." Justice officials in South Africa agreed, noting that donors have declined to fund criminal justice projects relating to victims' rights and other community needs. One advised that "donors must not stay rigidly locked into distinctions that exist only in their own manuals".

In Cambodia the same point was brought home to us by a women's human rights activist, who explained: "If we are to be true to the concern of the human rights movement for victims, justice reforms must be accompanied by a conscious effort to link human rights and security". In a country where those victimising women do not always wear a uniform, "the tendency to view these two concepts as somehow separate has the greatest negative impact on the most vulnerable in society, including women". Public support for protection of the human rights of criminal defendants is also at risk here. According to a Cambodian judge, "the 6 month limitation on pre-trial detention, coupled with the weak justice system, means, in practice, that dangerous criminals are released without trial, since the system lacks the facilities to build a case within that time. These criminals are free to prey on innocent Cambodians, who now live in fear in some areas". Police confirmed that the security situation is a problem in most of the country. In Phnom Penh, they said, it has improved since 1998, owing to gun confiscation, better policing of gangs and sensitive areas, and a fall in the number of kidnappings. However, people are still afraid to co-operate with the police, fearing retribution from kidnappers and gangs.

One answer, suggested in our discussions with beneficiaries in each of the four countries, may be a more conscious effort on the part of donors (and beneficiaries) to directly integrate human rights into programme support for security. It would help, for instance, to pay more attention in human rights programming to the importance of police, prosecutors and other security related institutions. Where this has occurred, it has all too often been restricted to teaching police and others about negative prohibitions (not to torture, etc.). The positive duties and obligations of protection which attach to state institutions under international human rights standards are often neglected in assistance programmes. If common understandings of security and human rights are to be linked, the positive role of security institutions in protecting personal security – in particular by defending women against rape, supporting victims of violent crime, and buttressing levels of community security – should be strengthened. At the same time, human rights safeguards protecting criminal defendants, prisoners, immigrants and others viewed unfavourably by the general public must be integrated from the start into plans for reform of the sector.

Six: EFFECTIVE AID RELATIONSHIPS

For beneficiaries the relationship between donor and beneficiary is crucial to the success of human rights assistance programmes. Many of our discussions focused upon identification of good and bad practice in this area. These exchanges highlighted a number of concerns, ranging from issues of ownership and transparency, to appropriate methodologies and types of aid.

Beneficiaries criticised donors who are not sufficiently attuned to local needs, and instead impose foreign models, or rely too heavily on foreign expertise. They value donors who are professional, not overly bureaucratic or formulaic in their approach. Donors that are accessible locally, are transparent and flexible in approach, and that (particularly for NGO beneficiaries) act in a spirit of solidarity are seen as more effective. Beneficiaries look for sustained commitment, and an appreciation that effective programmes will balance material and intellectual support. These and other points are developed in this chapter. Some key principles that emerge from this discussion are set out in the concluding chapter.

Local relationships

One donor official, active in the Cambodian justice sector and highly regarded by many of the government beneficiaries we met, explained how his team approached the relationship question. "We began with a needs assessment, consulting as much as possible. When the time came to start the project, we did not fly in and start giving orders or delivering lectures. Instead, the first six months that we were here were taken up by building relationships, listening, learning, and collecting information. By the time the everyday activities of the project were in full swing, we had established a mutual relationship of confidence and openness, based upon an agreed approach of confidentiality." NGO beneficiaries attached equal importance to a relationship of trust, noting that the success of projects in the sector often turned more on the people involved than on the methodology employed or even the funds granted.

Beneficiaries emphasised that aid work in the justice sector is sensitive and affects the lives and interests of beneficiaries far more than those of donors. "Get to know us. If you don't trust us, don't fund us. If you do, let us work, plan, judge. Listen to us, work with us, stay committed, avoid paternalistic approaches, and adopt one of solidarity instead." We heard repeatedly that donors who focus entirely on technical project management and administrative aspects, without due regard for the human side of development assistance (solidarity, trust, communication), were less effective. In other cases, we were told the heavily politicised "flavour" of some donors obstructed relationships of trust and solidarity.

Many, however, spoke highly of effective partnerships with donors who had successfully created relationships of solidarity and trust. Certain donors had come to be viewed by some NGOs as "part of the human rights community". Others were praised for their willingness and ability to respond flexibly to the needs of beneficiaries on the ground. Beneficiaries in the judiciary said they were convinced that the value of some judicial aid programmes was due largely to the collegial relationships around which they were constructed.

Some donors in Cambodia use intermediary organisations to channel their aid. Such organisations act as implementing or funding channels, situated locally and "between" the donor and the beneficiaries. A range of intermediary organisations are possible, ranging from local offices of intergovernmental bodies through private foundations established under national law – and under national control – that distribute aid from abroad. Their degree of autonomy from the agency that provides funds will vary. Beneficiaries saw important benefits in this approach on the grounds that intermediate organisations can:

- manage institutional bureaucracy;
- filter out the foreign policy bias of bilateral donors;
- "localise" activities and programmes (by hiring local personnel, and adjusting to the local context);
- increase domestic ownership (local staff, boards, advisory groups, and so on); and
- increase access to ongoing substantive advice, project management support, and flexible funding.

A number of such bodies have been established in Cambodia though beneficiaries said that some are more effective than others.[22] Personnel are a key factor. Beneficiaries told us that local implementing organisations should be staffed by competent nationals and internationals with expertise in local realities, human rights, and project management.

Beneficiary NGOs in South Africa also raised concerns about relationships. Their feelings were summed up neatly by one interviewee who said: "The best cases are those assistance providers which are decentralised, maintain a local presence, maximise the use of local personnel, include human rights specialists on staff, and provide flexible, solidarity based assistance." The worst cases were what another called "the North feeding neo-colonial directives to the South". A South African serving as project staff of a UN programme said he believed "good human rights assistance is present on the ground and flexible enough to respond to emerging local exigencies. It begins with a needs assessment, proceeds through basic start-up and capacity building, and sustains support

---

[22] Among them, the Cambodia Defenders Project of the International Human Rights Law Group, which will ultimately be spun off as a domestic organisation; the local Forum Syd office, representing a coalition of Swedish NGOs; and the local UN Office of the High Commissioner for Human Rights.

throughout implementation and consolidation". In South Africa, concerns like these have led donors to use intermediate organisations based locally, including a UN human rights office, a European Union Foundation, the Interfund consortium and others. These are intended to absorb donor bureaucracy, localise assistance, enhance the development relationship, and facilitate sustained support.

Guatemalan judges and justice officials also emphasised how important it is to use "the right people". A judge involved extensively in reform programmes told us that the success or failure of a project can turn entirely on the people managing the project and giving advice. He said that such advisers should be skilled and should work closely and in solidarity with domestic project partners. In Guatemala, too, some donors have developed "localised" ways to distribute their aid. Beneficiaries generally regarded such approaches favourably. For example, NOVIB (a Dutch organisation) works entirely through fully autonomous local organisations. The NGO consortium Project Consultancy Services (PCS) channels support from northern groups thorough its local office and operates under a local advisory council. The Soros Foundation, present since 1998, has committed itself to a ten-year presence and operates through a local board that includes Guatemalan experts and representatives of various ethnic and social groups. With a mission focused very much on "facilitation", Soros staff say they are "more interested in good ideas than in polished project proposals".

Bulgarian beneficiaries across the spectrum also appreciated the approach of private foundations with local offices. Many said that the Open Society Foundation was a model for an effective human rights assistance relationship. The qualities they listed included: a high degree of responsiveness to local realities, a high degree of domestic ownership, a high degree of flexibility, and a promise of sustained commitment. Bulgaria benefits from the presence of several intermediate organisations that channel aid from outside. Some have high levels of local ownership and control. In addition to the Open Society Foundation, there is the Centre for the Study of Democracy, supported by the Council of Europe, and the Democracy Network Programme, funded by USAID. Beneficiaries said that organisations of this sort allow a more direct relationship to develop and encourage continuous, face-to-face monitoring (in preference to more cumbersome and intrusive models). As a general rule, beneficiaries seemed to believe that decision-making and support should be located as close to beneficiaries as possible. They suggested that where donors could not themselves establish local offices they might channel support through others who were present.

We were warned though, that if intermediary organisations are not properly planned and staffed, they might evolve into "quasi-donors" rather than genuine local institutions connected to domestic constituencies. The key to success in the long-term, said some observers, is to develop local structures that are more democratic, more transparent, and more accountable.

Foreign models, expertise and interests

Is human rights assistance based upon local needs and the best interests of the beneficiaries, or the self-interest of the donors? Beneficiaries oppose what one described as the politicisation of assistance and, sometimes, the prioritising of donor self-interest over national human rights needs. They object to the imposition of foreign models, competition between donors, and the use of human rights assistance for the advancement of inconsistent foreign policy goals. Both government and NGO beneficiaries in the justice sector criticised the competition between donors and the imposition of foreign legal, judicial or policing models.

In Guatemala, one NGO representative told us: "We take one step forward and two steps back. Civilian police are finally established, the reform process gives us a chance to break with the past, and then donors come and structure the police around the model of the Spanish 'civil guards'. Whatever its value in Spain, this is a highly militarised model. Nothing could be more inappropriate for a country with Guatemala's history, and the remaining challenges of demilitarisation." [23] This view was shared by many in the human rights community. The imposition of foreign models was a charge made against other donors as well, including the United States. Beneficiaries felt that competition between proponents of US and Spanish policing models had created major difficulties. The two approaches differ in structure, emphasis and rules. A human rights specialist working in the justice sector explained that "we now have two largely incompatible influences in the development of Guatemalan law enforcement". Another worried that "police reform is already difficult and slow, due to internal resistance, an empowered old guard, and a lack of new blood. Donors complicate this by pushing their own models, and by pursuing their own interests". One donor interest being pursued, we were told, was a heavy emphasis on strengthening local capacity to fight drug trafficking. NGOs say that this distorted policing by creating more capacity to control drugs (an external priority) than to protect human rights (a Guatemalan priority).

Bulgarians, both in official institutions and NGOs, also wanted donors to cease promoting their national models. Donors have encouraged Bulgarian NGOS to apply to their own government for funding, a practice which (however valid in other countries) "would be the death of independence in the Bulgarian context". Official institutions in the sector also feel the effects of donor self-interest. Where police and prosecutors have received aid, for example, it has usually been for work on issues such as drugs, transnational crime, extradition, and stolen cars. A debate in the sector about appropriate models for a human rights institution (with

[23] This project, we were told, is an EU project which has been entrusted, at the request of the Guatemalan Government, to the Spanish Civil Guard (*Guardia Civil*).

the Council of Europe and France advocating an ombudsman, and the UN and some others a human rights commission) has left many beneficiaries unconvinced of the wisdom of either. In the end, said one Bulgarian observer, "the strongest lobby will win. The government is very sensitive to external pressure these days".

In Cambodia, donor self-interest has manifested itself in what observers describe as the open competition between various bilateral donors seeking to promote their own national models and systems. Foreign donor competition over whether Cambodia should have a civil or common law base to its legal system has been so fierce that some were reminded of the tensions between colonial powers earlier in the century. Some donors, entrusted with responsibility for developing draft codes, are said to have jealously guarded "their territory", preventing others from providing support and then failing to provide the promised outputs themselves. Others were accused of having so aggressively pushed their own national models as to have provoked open arguments with Cambodian judges and officials. One donor told us directly that their purpose in contributing to legal development was "to provide advice to Cambodians on our [the donor's] system and our laws". Local officials, involved in these activities since UNTAC's time, pointed out that these battles have continued since 1992, with predictable consequences. Officials who are not well-disposed towards reform can hide behind, or even manipulate, competition between different donor models to slow the reform process. In Cambodia, fundamental questions about the structure of the legal system, the conduct of trials, and the content of codes remain unresolved.

In the end, the Cambodian legal system has suffered most from this "code war". The country still operates under "temporary" UNTAC era codes, and lacks any comprehensive code of criminal procedure or national civil procedure. When we asked Cambodian officials to give their preference they replied: "We want new laws, responding to modern Cambodian realities, and based upon existing Cambodian law, UNTAC law, international standards and ASEAN requirements." Most simply wanted the legal gaps filled whatever the model, and appealed for better donor support to this end. Cambodia, which has decided not to establish its own law commission to do this work, owing to the absence of domestic legal and technical expertise, appears unable to resolve this issue without foreign support.

Some South African beneficiaries were also sceptical about the motivation of some donors. An experienced academic said the answer was to increase transparency, and use "filtering mechanisms" (i.e., funding UN projects, or implementing through NGO consortiums). "All ODA [overseas development assistance] has another agenda. This should therefore be clearly and publicly stated. Human rights assistance can have multiple purposes, to be sure, and donor self-interest is almost always among them." Beneficiaries, and sometimes donors themselves, affirmed that advancing human rights is seldom the sole goal of this assistance.[24] Those who provide human rights assistance and, in particular the bilateral government agencies, seek variously to create a climate for investment, to reduce migration, to increase their influence over developments in the country, to employ their own surplus of intellectual labour, to reduce the likelihood of drugs and transnational crime from reaching their borders, to collect intelligence, to influence local public opinion, and to advance an endless range of other foreign policy goals. Any benefits to the country receiving assistance, according to one South African, "are often incidental".

Beneficiary institutions in all four countries considered that tying aid to the use of donor country consultants and organisations, competitive bidding that pits local organisations against professional consultancy firms, or routine spending of the bulk of human rights assistance funds in the donor country, were inconsistent with the principles of capacity-building, local ownership, and transparency. The lack of authority of beneficiaries over donor-funded "experts" is a further problem, and beneficiaries point to the use of under-qualified consultants as a common result.

Most of the largest donors to the development of the justice sector in Cambodia, for example, implement through consultancy firms or NGOs from the donor country. They do not generally employ Cambodian organisations to manage programmes. They do so, apparently, for three reasons: express donor policy restrictions requiring the use of donor country institutions; practices of tendering and competitive bidding, which pit domestic bidders against sophisticated consulting firms in donor countries (sometimes dubbed "Belt-way Bandits" and "Brussels Bandits", for their proximity to and reliance on large donor funding sources); and the perceived absence of suitable alternatives in the country receiving assistance.

Beneficiaries made three points on this practice. The first concerned transparency. If the bulk of donor-funding earmarked for justice sector work in a beneficiary country was in fact absorbed by organisations and consultants in the donor country, beneficiaries asked if it was honest to register such funding as aid to the beneficiary. The second concerned capacity building. Continuous reliance on foreign expertise meant that local organisations would never develop their own capacity. Should resources spent in this fashion really be described as "aid"? The third concerned ownership. Was it appropriate or legitimate for foreign institutions to control the development of the justice sector in another country?

---

[24] Iris Almeida, Director, Rights and Democracy (in Montreal) pointed out that, in many countries today, the principal donor goal seems to be securing markets, rather than securing rights. "[...]Donor countries... are anxious to engage in trade and investment and are consequently eager to support the justice sector. Here the administration of justice becomes synonymous with "administration of contracts" and the promotion and protection of... human rights... takes a back seat." (*Communication to the Council*, 5 March 2000.)

Our discussions with beneficiaries suggested four criteria for evaluating the use of foreign expertise:

- its "added value" should justify the additional costs;
- priority should be given to the use of domestic institutions where possible, even if this meant arranging for a longer start-up phase designed to build domestic capacity;
- donors should clearly identify money spent on experts or organisations based in the donor country, and
- foreign experts should be subjected to evaluation, based upon consultation with beneficiaries.

In South Africa, beneficiaries said that it was both inappropriate and damaging to rely on foreign expertise where domestic organisations and experts were available. NGOs were the most adamant about this. "This approach causes divisions, erodes solidarity, weakens impact, and usurps our human rights heritage. In one way or another, we are forced to compete with consultants and NGOs in Sweden, Holland, Canada, the US, and others, when human rights assistance is supposed to be about building justice in South Africa. Whatever the merit of these foreign organisations, they cannot be said to have the same stakes as domestic institutions, or a constituency on the ground." South African NGOs also emphasised to us the importance of working with traditional leaders to advance the reform and development agenda. One organisation that is doing so in Kwazulu-Natal said that, to be effective, this work requires a deep understanding of the culture. "This means avoiding foreign formulae and methods, and trusting local implementers. This is not work that can reasonably be done by foreign consultants."

A Bulgarian official summed up the kind of resentment that can result from the misuse of foreign consultants. "The question to ask when deciding whether to appoint foreign experts is what will be the value added? Some donors send experts who stay for one or two years. They enter knowing nothing, learn all about us, then leave. We get very little. They get an education, huge salaries and expense accounts, and a law review article. And no one ever asks us to evaluate the work of the 'experts' they send to us." Many Bulgarian NGOs, while welcoming genuine alliances with groups in other countries, objected to the donor practice of requiring local institutions and organisations to take on donor country organisations as partners (for example, through twinning schemes).

Ownership, partnership and donor trends

A common complaint we heard from those who request assistance from donors was that donors "chase trends" or follow "fads" and emphasise quick fixes over solutions designed to respond to local needs, realities and aspirations. By this they mean that a particular issue or category for assistance becomes popular at international level and, for so long as this is so, support is available for the issue whether or not it is appropriate. Examples or "fads" people cited were child rights, economic and social rights, and national human rights commissions. One NGO activist told us that "donor trend-chasing causes chaos in the work and planning of the beneficiary organisations. The child rights trend has become an industry, with massive amounts of time and money spent on teaching child rights to children because it is non-threatening, while other critical areas are under-funded". Their point was that domestic priorities cannot be synchronised artificially with trends in donor agencies. One beneficiary said: "Setting priorities in human rights has to be based on a local determination of who is the most vulnerable, here and now."

South African beneficiaries also told us that donor "fads" complicate and can hinder human rights work. A woman working for an NGO explained that donors "often base everything on trends or partisan agendas (only child rights, only women's rights, etc.), with the effect that our work is artificially cut into little pieces". What was needed, we were told, was a "comprehensive approach" by sector. Beneficiaries believed that priorities and approaches had to be decided locally, based upon assessed needs. "We must be in a position to respond," said another, "whether the issue is a woman abused by her husband, or a farm-worker abused by the owner."

Bulgarian NGOs repeatedly raised the same issue with us, noting the disruptive effect that faddishness had on local human rights work. "Last year, we were suddenly required to all include economic and social rights references in our projects and reports," said a Bulgarian NGO officer. He thought this was superficial and asked: "Has this donor unilaterally decided that Bulgaria needs no specialised human rights institutions focusing on other human rights imperatives?"

Beneficiaries consistently argued that the role of human rights assistance is to support domestic reformers and domestic reform objectives. It should not be driven by the donor's vision of what is an appropriate institutional and social order. Successful reform, for almost all beneficiaries, implied local decision-making, local authority, local staffing, local ownership and local control. While specific local capacities will vary, externally supported projects and programmes should be designed with these principles and goals in mind. Beneficiaries also recognised that success, including successful local management of reform, requires donors and beneficiaries to share the same aims and objectives. This is an important safeguard, as is the full involvement of local human rights groups.

The lack of technical and professional expertise in Cambodia at the start of the 1990s (and almost total surrender of effective sovereignty in justice matters to foreigners during the UNTAC period) has had a profound impact on the relationship between donors and beneficiaries. Many beneficiaries we spoke to in

Cambodia acknowledged that donors had needed to be heavily involved in programme implementation early on, but felt they had failed to adjust as local capacity increased.

The Human Rights Action Committee, a coalition of human rights groups which convenes to respond to emerging human rights crises in Cambodia, said that donors have been supportive of the coalition's creative, action-oriented approach. Such support has been advisory as well as "political". Some worried, nevertheless, that donors had recently tried to participate in the body's substantive decision-making. They said this was inappropriate. In one case, which participants described as a direct assault on domestic ownership, donors threatened to cut funding if HRAC did not adopt the course of action they proposed. Some donors have taken important and, beneficiaries said, welcome steps toward increasing local ownership through the appointment of local project boards and advisory groups, by increasing numbers of national project staff, and by conducting consultative needs assessments. Respecting local ownership, said one Cambodian researcher, means respecting the whole picture and vision of a beneficiary's programme and avoiding piecemeal approaches.

Human rights organisations in South Africa worried that the tendency of donors to support specific activities rather than the general objectives and core costs of organisations they support can prevent beneficiaries from responding to emerging needs and crises and distort normal organisational development. The "pick and choose" approach means that programmes become donor-driven and therefore less legitimate. South Africans told us that this approach runs contrary to principles of democracy and self-determination. It substitutes donor objectives in place of the genuine needs and demands of the local constituencies to which beneficiary organisations are answerable. Some South African beneficiaries believed that certain donors refused to support efforts to obtain judicial remedies for abuses and encouraged reconciliation and conflict resolution approaches instead. They felt this was not an appropriate role for external actors to play. Some saw value in the appointment of local management or advisory boards, and maximising the use of national project staff to ensure greater local control over programmes. South Africans also warned, however, that superficial, checklist approaches to local or community ownership could be counterproductive. It was vital that this should be done with care and genuine consultation. The risk otherwise was that decision-making would simply be surrendered to those who were already more powerful, such as government officials (over civil society), landlords (over tenants), men (over women), the wealthy (over the poor) and so on.

Evolution

Beneficiaries appreciated donors who evolved and adapted their programmes as national partners increased their capacity and the context changed. The normal trend should be away from heavy donor involvement in implementation and oversight, and, through capacity-building, towards more autonomy for domestic institutions.

In Cambodia, aid to the justice sector has been heavily affected by "the UNTAC factor". There was an enormous and sudden injection of aid during the 18-month presence of Cambodia's peacekeeping operation. Much of it was *ad hoc* in nature. Donors managed many of the country's institutions. Relatively little effort was made to build their capacity, particularly in the official sector. Together, these factors slowed domestic institutional development and frustrated domestic ownership.

Cambodian NGOs argued that donors should phase their support, develop capacity, and gradually grant partners more freedom and autonomy. The Cambodia office of Oxfam-UK, whose programme includes support for human rights activities, adopted such an approach. Opened in 1979 to carry out emergency and relief work with the government, it later took on a longer-term development role as needs changed. In 1991, it began to employ Khmer staff, and later still ceased to implement and became a donor to local NGOs. Today, the programme supports [25] local partners working on human rights issues.

Many South African beneficiaries also emphasised that donor policies needed to evolve. However, some said that South Africa illustrated a kind of reverse evolution, because aid providers were more flexible, more empowering and more trusting during the *apartheid* era (before 1994), and had become much more rigid, bureaucratic and controlling since then. Some beneficiaries believed that donors deserve credit for their willingness to "loosen the reins" during the *apartheid* years, and that it is appropriate to introduce more stringent local management now. They added however, that it makes little sense to reduce the autonomy of organisations that have proven capacity.

Bulgarian human rights organisations thought that donors are better equipped to handle the requirements of beneficiary institutions at the beginning of reform processes, and that they deal less well with subsequent phases. One representative noted that "donors seem less able to respond to the changing needs of beneficiaries as the situation evolves". In later stages, when issues become more complex, the actors more diverse, and the needs more varied, "assistance providers often fail to adjust to the new realities". They believed donors should be responsive to emerging realities and to increasing capacities. As the capacity of an organisation increases, so too should its autonomy.

[25] This is not to say that these NGOs objected to the idea of multiple sources of funding. To the contrary, we were told it acts to safeguard independence (both real and perceived).

Transparency

Both government and NGO beneficiaries agreed that clear, complete and accessible information on the assistance that donors provide should be made available to the institutions and communities they support. We were told, however, this was rarely the case. Some donors operated in "a shroud of secrecy" and provided little information about their activities, procedures, and budgets. Others, said beneficiaries who had been subject to project and programme evaluations, did not always provide the results of evaluations they conducted. Having attempted to obtain such information ourselves, we can confirm that basic documents on donor programmes are often unavailable in the beneficiary country. According to a Bulgarian NGO representative: "Transparency is not just a matter of good will on the part of the donor. It requires planning, and specific measures written into project frameworks."

There are, however, cases where lack of transparency is intentional. In some instances donors refused to provide information in order to protect human rights groups that they funded. This was the case in South Africa and Guatemala, where, prior to the commencement of current reforms, non-governmental human rights groups were seen as subversive organisations by their governments. However, most beneficiaries suggested (and donors seemed to agree) that donors should be transparent wherever conditions permit.

Flexibility and responsiveness

Working in an often unpredictable and rapidly evolving political and social environment, beneficiaries place a high premium on flexibility in the aid relationship. The extent to which relationships are responsive to changing beneficiary needs is an important factor in success.

Delays in delivery, unreasonable bureaucratic requirements, and the pervasiveness of a "project management culture" devoid of human rights substance, were major shortcomings identified, especially by NGOs. Here, some drew sharp distinctions between different donors. They said some were true partners who responded flexibly to needs as they emerged. But there was strong criticism of donors who were overly bureaucratic and unresponsive. Beneficiaries, especially NGOs dependent on grants to fund their activities, recognised that most of their work would be impossible without donors to fund it, but wanted those donors to acknowledge and show more understanding of the constraints they operated under.

Many donors limit the grant they will provide to an organisation (25% to 30% of its budget for some, 50% for at least one). Several will support the costs of projects only, refusing to fund core operating costs. Most do not cover staffing costs. In this environment, active organisations must maintain a financial relation with several donors. For small organisations especially, doing so can be overwhelming. "We have to provide up to three reports per year to some donors.

If you multiply that times seven donors, you see why we need a full time staff member just to satisfy donor requirements. Add to that the fact that we work in the local language, but have to provide information materials and reports in English to the donors," remarked one NGO representative.[25]

Beneficiaries offered many recommendations for improving donor practice here. They advised donors to decentralise and localise their operations; provide clear and continuous information on their requirements, objectives, approach, and functioning; have people in their office who know the country, and know the substance of human rights and justice administration; provide technical support to help beneficiaries meet the application, reporting, accounting, and other requirements of donors; and offer capacity-building support to beneficiary organisations and institutions. Many beneficiaries also appealed for more co-ordination of donor language, categories, reporting requirements and procedures.

Of course, donors must ensure that beneficiaries account properly for aid they receive. None of the beneficiaries we met objected to financial oversight, sound management procedures, or reporting as such. Most agreed that proper accountability strengthened rather than weakened beneficiary organisations. Their objections were to disproportionate administrative burdens imposed by donors that detract attention from domestic constituencies and reduce the beneficiary's overall efficiency. "At some point," said one, "you cease to be an organisation serving domestic needs, and become one serving donor needs."

Some beneficiaries said that project management methodology is important and can increase the technical capacity of the beneficiary. Properly applied, it provides a common reference point for donors and beneficiaries, and allows beneficiaries to make objective decisions about what donors are doing. Seen from this perspective, it can be empowering. Staff of one South African human rights organisation, which is still struggling to transform itself from a "largely white, liberal anti-*apartheid* organisation" into one more representative of the community, believed that such methodology was playing a crucial role in ensuring that decisions are more objective, more performance-based and less arbitrary. In general, South African beneficiaries welcomed financial project audits and responsible management requirements. The problem, some told us, was that project management methodology was too often badly applied by donors, was interpreted too rigidly, involved unnecessary red tape, or was applied in such a way that donors could not adapt as situations changed. NGO beneficiaries described one major donor as "focused entirely on its own preconceived programme objectives and administrative concerns, to the extent that local realities and needs are viewed as unwelcome complications". This was especially problematic where providers were not present locally, or where staff were not familiar with the local context or unable to communicate skills in project management.

Sound methodology

Assistance to the justice sector has a direct impact on vital institutions and matters of public interest. For obvious reasons programmes should be implemented and evaluated professionally. According to beneficiaries, this has not always been the case. Some assistance programmes to the justice sector have served to train young northern lawyers. Others have been used to test undeveloped methodologies. Generally speaking, beneficiaries said they have little opportunity to control the quality of assistance programmes. In some cases, the limited capacity of domestic institutions means that beneficiaries are not aware of best practices. In others, the uneven power balance between the two sides is such that beneficiaries avoid criticising aid that is of poor quality.

When asked, however, many had serious concerns about these issues. Cambodian judges and other justice officials, for example, said they had rarely been consulted by donor teams conducting needs assessments, project evaluations, or planning exercises, and most were not made aware that these were taking place. They expressed concern about inexperienced foreign advisers, about the highly general and often irrelevant content of training and advice, and about the failure of providers to help build the capacity of their institutions.

Some also believed that donors tried to "force bridge-building methods on human rights building activities". There were those who still measured success by whether or not the project budget was spent on time. Bulgarians insisted that arbitrariness in donor programmes had created, or exacerbated domestic divisions. Bad methodology, whether for project management, training approaches, grant making, or any other aspect of human rights assistance, will tend to damage domestic institutions and retard domestic reforms.[26] Beneficiaries in South Africa and Guatemala offered a common piece of advice for donors: focus on the process, not the project. One beneficiary told us that a major donor evaluated the programmes of six organisations in two weeks. "There is a lot of 'going through the motions'", she concluded.

The right balance: advice and funds

Justice sector reforms have both technical and physical implications. Effective human rights assistance must address both. Advice will not enable impoverished justice systems to meet all the requirements of international human rights standards. Financial and material aid will not by themselves create institutions that are willing to reform. Beneficiaries wanted development relationships that balance the need for ideas and the need for dollars. Particularly in the justice sectors of developing countries whose central institutions and functions cannot be

---

[26] With regard to training, beneficiaries and donors alike wanted better ways to measure the impact of training, though they were aware that this cannot be done in the short term. Sonny Ostberg, Cambodia Field Director for ForumSyd, explained that useful measures can be applied in the form of questionnaires and follow up contact with trainees. (*Communication to the Council*, 29 February 2000.)

contracted to private firms or NGOs, support for core costs can mean the difference between fair and humane justice administration, or bottlenecks, miscarriages of justice and abuse.

While justice officials themselves often said that training and technical advice is the most pressing need in their sector, they also made the point that international standards have resource implications. Many standards would be difficult to respect if new resources are not committed to infrastructure. They mentioned several examples: the need to build adequate judicial facilities, including separate courts for juveniles; the need to ensure humane prison conditions; and the need to provide non-lethal police equipment. The cost implications of reform, they pointed out, are unavoidable.

On the other hand, some Guatemalans worried that certain donor projects were too heavily focused on the "hardware" of buildings and equipment, without sufficient linkages to actual reforms. "All the buildings and equipment in the world will not help," we were told, "when the central problem is, after all, impunity." Bulgarian human rights activists added that the important point was to provide an appropriate balance, and to link assistance, whether financial or technical, to specific reforms, and not just to institutions. There is no general ratio to fix the balance between ideas and dollars, and therefore no substitute for careful national consultation, study and assessment.

Sustained commitment

Justice sector reform is, necessarily, a long-term process. It is not just about setting up new institutions, or reforming old ones, but about changing how people think – about recognising the value of rights and their enforcement. The implication for donors, we were told, is that they must take a long-term view, support long-term projects, and stay the course through inevitable periods of instability. Beneficiaries across the spectrum believed that donors should stay engaged in the reform process in spite of (indeed, sometimes because of) political crises, slow progress, or critical events in other countries. Beneficiaries accused some donors of chasing headlines ("Bosnia today, Timor tomorrow"), cutting human rights assistance in one country in order to shift attention and resources to another. This is not an unrealistic fear. At least two donors with whom we spoke confirmed that the events in Kosovo in 1999 were likely to cause a reduction in funding for human rights assistance in Cambodia. On the other side, Bulgarians were told to expect a reprieve from previously expected donor cuts; events in Kosovo had once again put the spotlight on democratic reform in the region.

Many beneficiaries were convinced that "on-again, off-again" aid made planning impossible and advancement of reforms more difficult. They felt the focus of some donors on "exit strategies" distracted development agendas away from the work at hand, as beneficiaries struggle, compete and despair in the face of imminent cut-offs. The tendency to support one-off activities (such as *ad hoc* training courses), rather than long-term institutions (such as universities, judicial training institutions, and police academies), is also wasteful and unsustainable.

A Cambodian human rights defender explained his view of the importance of sustaining human rights assistance: "The authoritarian regimes in the region are watching Cambodia's democratic experiment. If it fails, they will tell their people '...you see? Cambodia tried the western model of human rights and democracy and look where it brought them'". According to him, if Cambodia succeeds, it will set the course for Vietnam, Laos, and others, even China. "Human rights and democracy for this region turns on the success or failure of the Cambodia experiment. These are the stakes. And the Cambodia experiment is squarely in the hands of the NGOs at this point. If they fail, human rights and democracy will fail. Donors must take heed of this message: remain vigilant, avoid complacency, sustain the commitment, recognise the stakes, and improve support for the democratic experiment in Cambodia."

Beneficiaries also believed that most so-called "exit strategies" are likely to fail. Every country, every justice system, every national political and economic situation is different. For this reason, explained one NGO representative: "Exit strategies by donors can never be preconceived. The situation on the ground, rather than some donor capital formula, must dictate the appropriate level of donor commitment. In fragile periods of transition, there is no moral alternative to sustained commitment." Others agreed, pointing out that there are simply no domestic funding sources in many countries for human rights monitoring and investigations, or for advocacy on behalf of prisoners. They argued that the cost of exit, from a human rights perspective, would be morally unimaginable.

NGO beneficiaries made the point that some donors are confused about the notion of "sustainability". They define it as the ability to continue after the cut-off of external funding. Much work done by human rights NGOs in poor countries fails that test. "This is incorrect," we were told by a Cambodian activist. "Our programmes have sustainable impact (people are trained, elected, laws are transformed). But no non-governmental human rights organisation can really hope to survive in the current Cambodian context without donor support." The donor tendency to emphasise financial sustainability obfuscates the fuller picture. Sustainability should include technical, political, and physical sustainability, as well as social sustainability (such as the public adoption of human rights or democratic values).

Beneficiaries also questioned donors who look for short-term indicators of success. We were told that real progress in reform of the justice sector cannot be measured quantitatively in the short or medium term. "In this area," we heard, "you cannot make short-term, concrete promises based on specific measures, when the subject matter and related issues of causation are so complex." What is more, donors working in this sector are bound to become frustrated and tempted to disengage if they are judged against traditional notions of impact measurement. "Some donors are so obsessed with looking for short-term results that they resent the product of our monitoring activities," said representatives of a leading NGO. "Some want us to 'stop complaining', sometimes claiming that we are too negative, painting an overly grim picture, presumably to sustain our own interests. They need to learn not to shoot the messenger if the news is bad. This is the state of human rights, this is reality, and this is our job." Another added: "cutting funding for monitoring may well stop the reports, but it won't stop the violations".

Some South African beneficiaries said that the increasing donor talk of "exit strategies" was strategically unwise, and had the potential to jeopardise the success or sustainability of reforms in some institutions. Such talk is also considered to be inconsistent. "Once you get involved, create expectations, and push reforms, you have an obligation to stay involved at least through implementation and into the consolidation phase of the process. The rush to exit by some donors now is morally unjustifiable after decades of western support for the institutions of *apartheid* and the frustration of South African democracy." Nor, said South African NGOs, do short-term "packages" and *ad hoc* activities make sense in the context of justice reforms. "Institution-building for justice requires a long-term focus. It does not lend itself to short-term projects, short-term indicators, and donor conceptions of instantly 'realisable targets'."

An indigenous human rights defender in Guatemala observed that "some donors think that the genocide ended with the signing of the peace accords and the start of reform projects. But genocide is not resolved in the length of a project cycle". Others shared the concern that human rights assistance is sometimes approached as a short-term matter. A jurist in the country believed that donors had significant influence over the direction and shape of reforms, and yet "do not always recognise the long term nature of justice reform". This, he said, was evident in the multitude of short term training courses offered, and the paucity of support for long term institutions, like permanent training centres, academies and law schools. Government beneficiaries agreed. One Guatemalan official told us that real transformation will come only with the injection of "new blood", as existing judges and justice officials are all products of the old system. This necessarily implies the need for support to be directed to universities and law schools that create new lawyers, "not only to seminars to try to convert the old". At least one donor in Guatemala seems to have absorbed the message of sustained commitment. "Rule of law assistance is not a straight-line sprint to the finish line, as some donors seem to think," he said. "Rather it is a dance, moving back, forward, left, right, then forward again. It requires both partners to move together, and to stick it out until the music is finished."

Beneficiaries in Bulgaria were also concerned by the donors' emphasis on "exit strategies" and cut-off dates. Many made the point that effective human rights assistance requires a more sustained commitment by donors. Instead, all too often, "everything is framed in 'temporariness'. The emphasis is not on sustained commitment or careful institution building, but on projects measured in months, and on exit dates". The same Bulgarian human rights activist explained further that "this creates mess, panic, waste, corruption and hidden agendas on all sides. It comes to define the strategies of both donors and beneficiaries. In the end, the agenda becomes distorted, as all are focused on the day when the donor will depart, rather than on what will be left behind". Most recently, said NGO beneficiaries, donors have focused on "alternative funding", which presumes that NGOs will find local support to pick up where donors leave off. Many have been advised to seek funding from the government, from the general public, or from local business. Most Bulgarians consider this is entirely unrealistic. NGO beneficiaries pointed out that the recent history of Bulgaria makes it inappropriate for NGOs to seek funds from their own governments (an approach advocated by donors from Western European countries with a social democratic tradition). They felt it would jeopardise their independence. Likewise, they said, the local business community would impose unacceptable conditions on funding. As for the general public, "poor, struggling and lacking a tradition of civic participation, [t]hey are unlikely to give their bread money to a human rights organisation". One Bulgarian human rights activist summed up the situation in terms equally applicable to many countries: "If the donors do exit, it will not be the human rights organisations that survive here. What we are selling is not the most marketable of products: minority rights in a racist society; prisoner rights in an insecure society; women's rights in a traditional society."

How long is the long-term?

The implications for donor support are clear – assistance should be provided for the long-term. But donor agencies might legitimately respond: how long is that? In the real world, it may be unreasonable to expect assistance to continue indefinitely. Donors have other constituencies, other responsibilities. Moreover, both NGO and official institutions in receipt of aid have a duty to aim to be self-sustaining. Some would argue, in relation to NGOs, that continued reliance on foreign support may inadvertently strengthen views in the country that human rights are a foreign import. One response of beneficiaries to such arguments, at least as regards official bilateral aid, was to point to the fact that in some cases the repressive machinery that is being replaced was itself sustained (or even established) by foreign support (political, economic and military) over many decades. In that period, there was little talk of "exit strategies".

Yet, for donors the problem of long-term support remains a difficult one. It would seem that, at a minimum, donor agencies should not make major commitments that they cannot complete, nor encourage organisations and institutions to plan for support that is unlikely to materialise. Also, there are cases where foreign support to NGOs provides a degree of protection and legitimacy that, were it withdrawn, would put in jeopardy not simply the organisation, but the freedom and security of its staff. Most would agree talk of "exit strategies" is inappropriate in such cases.

Foreign support for independent justice institutions

Independence is essential to the function of many institutions in the justice sector. Judges, human rights commissions, some police oversight mechanisms, and, to a degree, defence lawyers and prosecutors are all required to be independent. In relation to human rights assistance, this raises two fundamental questions. Does foreign assistance jeopardise independence? Is institutional independence a barrier to reform? In our discussions, most beneficiaries answered no to both questions. Of course, the independence of judiciaries, statutory commissions, and other justice sector institutions must be respected by donors and governments alike. But such independence, we were told, should not be threatened by – or be used to obstruct – externally supported reforms.

Guatemalan lawyers perceived no conflict between donor-supported reforms and judicial independence. One who was involved in the reform process insisted that reform is in the public interest and should not be blocked by judges on the grounds of their "independence". NGOs and government officials broadly agreed. Guatemalan judges, however, had another point of view. Reform advocates pointed to several recent instances when judges had blocked reform on the grounds that it would undermine the independence of the judiciary. In one case, an attempt was made (rather ironically) to block a visit by the UN Rapporteur on the Independence of the Judiciary because it would compromise their independence. In another, judges claimed that World Bank loans and projects for justice reform would threaten judicial independence. In a third, judges resisted wider participation in justice sector co-ordination on the same grounds.

A Bulgarian judge told us that human rights assistance did not threaten judicial independence. She saw such arguments as a smoke-screen that individual judges or officials used to oppose reform. "Donors and advisers are not parties in a case before the bench, and assistance projects are forward-looking rather than retrospective. They cannot therefore threaten independence, properly understood." By mid-1999, efforts had begun to integrate and co-ordinate justice reform by establishing a board on which judicial representatives would sit with other actors from the justice sector to plan and implement a donor-supported judicial reform initiative.

In Cambodia, none of the beneficiaries to whom we spoke, including the judges, considered judicial independence to be threatened by the involvement of external donors. Some defence lawyers were of a different mind, however. Members of the Bar Association recalled that in one case foreign funding of the organisation was made conditional on their agreeing not to represent certain defendants (in this case, members of the Khmer Rouge). The Bar Association declined the grant because they felt acceptance of the condition would have been a breach of legal ethics. A full understanding of human rights would recognise the importance of ensuring *any* defendant was given the chance for a proper defence.

South African beneficiaries also argued that human rights assistance does not compromise judicial independence. The new Constitutional Court, for example, benefited from a court trust fund, a mechanism that allows the court to use donor support while maintaining its own agenda and insulating its work from external influence. South African lawyers, officials and legal scholars recalled, nevertheless, that some overseas experts from countries with long developed justice systems have emphasised "independence" at the expense of other judicial principles. In South Africa's context, they felt that might well delay reform. In the difficult process of transforming a judiciary formed under apartheid, an exaggerated emphasis on independence might help to entrench and shelter procedures and judicial officials who are opposed to reform. "Judicial independence is vital," said one beneficiary, "but, in the context of transition, so are accountability and progress."

In sum, beneficiaries said the key is to balance the requirement of independence with the need to reform justice systems so that they effectively protect human rights.

The relevance of international human rights standards

Conflicts over appropriate legal standards seem to occur all too frequently in the context of donor supported justice sector reforms. Donor foreign policy objectives, advocacy of foreign models, and the imposition of foreign experts can all potentially conflict with the human rights objective of justice sector assistance and with local visions of the best way to achieve those objectives. It is natural that donors have their own interests; but where these conflict with local human rights objectives, beneficiaries argue that the latter must be paramount. International human rights standards should provide a common normative basis for the donor-beneficiary relationship in human rights assistance. These standards apply regardless of a country's particular legal system. They should replace imported national models and obviate donor competition over them.

Many of the officials we interviewed in the focus countries believed that international standards were a good starting point for development of new domestic laws and institutions. NGOs agreed, adding that a focus on international standards creates a common normative thread around which to co-ordinate the various beneficiary and donor institutions. Others insisted that use of international standards is "the best way to overcome sensitivities to criticism and political concerns". Some donors, especially intergovernmental organisations (such as the UN or the Council of Europe), do base their advice and support on international standards together with existing local laws. Others rely too heavily on their own national laws and models.

The conflicts evident between donors about use of their own national models suggest that more attention could be given to the comprehensive and detailed administration of justice standards developed by the UN and regional organisations (such as the Council of Europe and the Organisation of American States). Some beneficiaries believed lack of attention to international standards would erode their authority. In Guatemala, where judges resisted a visit of the UN Special Rapporteur on the Independence of the Judiciary on highly nationalistic "sovereignty" grounds, a government official thought donors should share the blame. "Donors have pushed their own models and laws for so long, and ignored international standards so totally, that beneficiaries involved in justice reforms nationally are ignorant of international norms, and therefore resist them."

International human rights standards, particularly those adopted under UN auspices, do in fact provide a detailed normative framework for justice administration, as well as justice reform and development. While the instruments will be obvious to human rights specialists, they may be less familiar to others. They include treaties, declarations, guidelines and bodies of principles.[27] While these standards do not answer every problem of legal reform, they offer a sound way to ensure reforms pay due regard to human rights.

[27] A list of relevant UN standards includes: Universal Declaration of Human Rights; International Covenant on Civil and Political Rights; International Covenant on Economic, Social and Cultural Rights; UN Standard Minimum Rules for the Treatment of Prisoners; UN Basic Principles for the Treatment of Prisoners; UN Body of Principles for the Protection of All Persons under Any Form of Detention or Imprisonment; UN Rules for the Protection of Juveniles Deprived of their Liberty; UN Declaration on the Protection of All Persons From Being Subjected to Torture and Other Cruel, Inhuman or Degrading Treatment or Punishment; UN Convention against Torture and Other Cruel, Inhuman or Degrading Treatment or Punishment; UN Safeguards Guaranteeing Protection of the Rights of those Facing the Death Penalty; UN Code of Conduct for Law Enforcement Officials; UN Basic Principles on the Use of Force and Firearms by Law Enforcement Officials; UN Basic Principles on the Role of Lawyers; UN Guidelines on the Role of Prosecutors; UN Standard Minimum Rules for Non-Custodial Measures; UN Guidelines for the Prevention of Juvenile Delinquency; UN Standard Minimum Rules for the Administration of Juvenile Justice; UN Declaration of Basic Principles of Justice for Victims of Crime and Abuse of Power; UN Basic Principles on the Independence of the Judiciary; UN Declaration on the Protection of All Persons from Enforced Disappearance; UN Principles on the Effective Prevention and Investigation of Extra-Legal, Arbitrary and Summary Executions. The full text of each of these instruments can be found in United Nations, *Human Rights: A Compilation of International Instruments*, Vol. I (First Part), Universal Instruments, (UN Doc. ST/HR/1/Rev.5), UN New York and Geneva, 1994.

Seven: **CONCLUSIONS AND FINDINGS**

Beneficiaries believe that human rights assistance to the justice sector, properly provided, can and has had an important impact. This said, success depends in large measure on the degree to which human rights are integrated into the development process as a whole; on the adoption of a strategic approach; on the establishment of effective and honest partnerships that recognise the authority of beneficiaries to direct reform efforts; and on careful attention to challenges that particularly affect the justice sector.

In all the countries visited, the beneficiaries to whom we spoke claimed that justice sector aid programmes have been useful. They have facilitated constitutional development and legislative reform, and helped expand civil society, transformed the justice system and brought about other beneficial institutional changes. In a short period, helped by these programmes, concepts of human rights have been introduced into the public consciousness and public institutions in societies where such notions were once seen as subversive or even treasonous. Beneficiaries pointed to the unparalleled democratic transition evident across the globe during the last decade of the 20th century, and insisted that these achievements could not have occurred without the support of international donors. From this angle, human rights assistance has undoubtedly been effective.

However, beneficiaries were equally clear that poor assistance can do harm, and that some programmes have hindered the promotion and protection of human rights. Badly conceived and implemented programmes have sheltered repressive regimes from scrutiny, wasted vital resources, distorted domestic institutions and fostered social division. It was widely claimed that donors sometimes promote alien and inappropriate models and put their foreign policy interests before human rights and development objectives. Some are unreliable partners – subject to whims of policy, quick fixes and an inappropriate focus on "exit strategies" – undermining the effectiveness and sustainability of programmes they themselves sought to promote.

Human rights assistance for justice reform is not a miracle cure, but neither is it a mere placebo. It is one tool that – when it is used effectively – can reduce tyranny and impunity and improve democracy and the rule of law. Some of the steps that need to be taken to make human rights assistance more effective are set out in the findings that follow.

FINDINGS

I. The beneficiary perspective

No programme of human rights assistance will accomplish meaningful change, or be sustainable after the departure of the aid provider, if it is conceived or imposed from abroad. Ultimately, national institutions and organisations must take charge of reform processes in their societies and guide the direction of external assistance for those reforms. Effective participation by beneficiaries in aid programmes is a necessary (though not sufficient) condition of their success.

Justice reform efforts that do not have the support of beneficiaries, or for which beneficiaries do not take responsibility, will not be legitimate, effective or sustainable.

II. Human rights and development

Aid to the justice sector would be more effective if the relation between human rights and development was more clearly understood and integrated in policy and practice. There are clear links between underdevelopment, poverty and poorly-functioning justice systems. Building justice systems that are effective – that protect human rights – requires a commitment to reform. Successful reform requires national organisations and donors to assemble, and put to use, the range of material, technical and intellectual resources that are vital to the functioning of justice systems.

More and more institutions involved in development are adopting a rights-based approach. Among other things, such an approach emphasises the legal enforcement of claims, the importance of institutions and laws to deliver on those claims, and attention to issues of discrimination and poverty – to ensure that development benefits all sectors of the population. Such an approach is closely linked to justice sector reform and could strengthen the impact of aid.

Such an approach further emphasises the right of the public, who are the ultimate beneficiaries of aid, to participate in the development of their societies and its institutions.

III. Threshold issues: when to engage and with whom?

Human rights assistance is a useful tool in most political environments, including ones that are imperfect, in which governments do not protect rights well. Human rights aid should not generally be withheld except in cases where the government concerned *explicitly* rejects and blatantly violates international human rights standards. Donors will remain anxious about providing assistance to countries that have a poor human rights record. However, the risks that donors incur by providing aid are outweighed by the support they give to those working locally for reform. Reform of a justice system cannot be achieved quickly or smoothly. Donors should expect to make a long-term commitment.

- *Identify reform constituencies.* Governments are complex institutions. Aid can be provided usefully to individual reformers and specific institutions even when the government, as a whole, is resistant to change. In cases where commitment to reform is very weak, civil society organisations, national human rights institutions and reformist parliamentarians can be helpful. In a few cases it is appropriate to channel aid to official institutions through national and international NGOs. In general, aid to strengthen non-official institutions should not displace aid to strengthen official institutions.

- *High threshold for aid cut-offs.* While donors have an obligation to avoid complicity, they should avoid abandoning reformers when they most need international support. Beneficiaries set a high threshold for cutting off human rights assistance to the justice sector. Aid should not be cut without first consulting local opinion, including the opinion of reformers and human rights organisations.

- *Human rights monitoring AND assistance.* It is not inconsistent to monitor violations of human rights and to provide aid at the same time. The two activities can complement one another. Human rights assistance cannot be done well without good information concerning the human rights situation in the country, and this requires monitoring. Whether donors should report publicly their concerns will depend on the situation. Donors with an explicit human rights mandate – like the UN – cannot be silent. The guiding principle for donors is consistency in what they say and do.

- *Engage the official sector.* Donors are often reluctant to engage fully with official institutions because they do not wish to be criticised for assisting or associating with abusive organisations. This attitude can slow the progress of reform. Since justice is a responsibility of the state, donors who seek seriously to support reform of the justice sector must involve themselves in the reform of official institutions. Indeed, support to reformers in official institutions is likely to be especially important where the political environment is least favourable to reform. Aid in this area involves donors in political risk, which donors should shoulder alongside local reformers, who may be even more exposed.

- *Go beyond "safe aid".* Donors tend not to assist institutions, such as prisons, prosecutors and police, which are not popular or bring higher risks. They tend to prefer to assist "safer" institutions, such as national commissions and NGOs. Similarly, they tend to prefer to fund less controversial activities such as training courses, and to avoid riskier projects, such as the purchase of police security equipment. In practice, this is often unfavourable to effective reform.

IV. Strategic approaches

Much assistance for justice reform has been poorly planned and co-ordinated.

Reforms would be more effective if both donors and beneficiaries adopted a more strategic approach. At national level, clear national policies and plans should be formulated. Donors should assist these efforts. They should co-ordinate their activities better, avoid duplication, and improve their understanding of local needs.

Beneficiaries said that a more strategic approach might include the following elements:

- *Recognise that justice is a sector (like other development sectors).*
  National governments and donors should think of justice as a sector, as they think of health, education and agriculture. This would enable them to link together the many roles that different official and non-official institutions and actors play in justice reform.

- *Include civil society groups in the justice sector.* Civil society organisations, including human rights NGOs and lawyers' organisations, play essential roles in the delivery of justice and in planning, implementing and monitoring reform and assistance programmes.

- *State clear policy commitments.* Justice sector reforms stand a better chance of success when the government has a clearly-stated policy. This should set out overall objectives and the reforms that will be introduced to achieve them. Such policies may be grounded in a peace agreement or a new constitution or a national plan. Whatever their form, they provide a foundation for coherent action. Donors can usefully assist efforts to develop such policies.

- *Prepare specific plans for the justice sector.* The actions of national institutions and donors are more likely to be effective and coherent if detailed plans for reform of the justice sector have been prepared. Ideally, such plans should be developed nationally, in a participatory way that involves public consultation including consultation with institutions active in the justice sector. Such plans should set clear benchmarks, and frame reform as a process rather than a single event. Here too, donors can assist such efforts.

- *Monitor the progress of reform.* Both beneficiaries and donors need clear and reliable information, about projects that are underway and about the assistance that donors are providing. Such information should be gathered regularly and made available. The surveys should enable beneficiaries and donors to determine (in relation to overall reform objectives) what has been done, what is already planned, and what remains to be addressed.

- *Require participatory needs assessment.* Many human rights aid programmes are undertaken without assessing needs and capacities in advance. This is not good development practice and is not helpful to successful reform. Beneficiaries should be consulted whenever needs are assessed.

- *Improve co-ordination.* Reform projects in the justice sector have not generally been co-ordinated well. Both donors and beneficiaries have responsibility for weaknesses in this area. Reform plans should address the issue of co-ordination. Co-ordination should be led by the government (wherever feasible), and include the participation of civil society organisations.

V. Justice reform safeguards

The needs of poor, vulnerable and marginalised groups should be given priority when planning, implementing and monitoring reform of the justice sector.

- *Ensure access to justice.* Access to justice is a crucial issue. Reform strategies should seek to remove barriers of class, race, gender, language, religion and geography. The success of reform should be judged (in part) on whether official institutions tackle discrimination effectively and are accessible to poor and excluded members of the society.
- *Recognise indigenous systems.* Minorities and indigenous populations should be involved in the reform process, including especially decisions that will affect them. Indigenous legal systems and traditions should be formally recognised in law and accommodated appropriately in the legal system.
- *Empower women.* Special attention should be paid to the rights of women. This is best achieved through locally-developed strategies designed to increase women's empowerment and participation, and strengthening the capacity of justice systems to protect women from discrimination and violence (including domestic abuse, rape and trafficking) that are gender-specific.
- *Involve minorities.* Wherever feasible, donors should assist organisations that articulate the interests of minority groups – including organisations formed by and composed of such groups. Support should build the capacity of these organisations, and seek to empower members of minority communities.
- *Link human rights and security.* It is difficult to sustain support for human rights reform in societies where personal security is not assured. It is therefore important to ensure that the reform process emphasises the positive duties of police, prosecutors and courts to protect the rights of victims, women, and the general public, and that strong safeguards remain in place to protect prisoners, migrants and other unpopular groups.
- *Institutional independence.* Aid should not undermine the independence of judiciaries, statutory commissions, and other justice sector institutions. The requirement of independence, however, should not obstruct reforms that are designed to enable judicial institutions to operate in accordance with international human rights standards. An independent judiciary is important but, where judicial institutions are weak, discriminatory or defective, reform is essential.

VI. Effective aid relationships

The relationship between donor and beneficiary is crucial to the success of human rights assistance programmes. For both, key principles include a commitment to:

- *Transparency.* Hidden agendas, whether real or imagined, inhibit the trust that is essential to effective aid partnerships. Information on the reform process and on all aspects of donor assistance should be readily accessible to the public and to the various parties actively involved. Some donors do not make enough information available about their work.

- *Sustained commitment.* Successful reform requires sustained commitment from governments, national institutions and donors. Donors need to treat reform as a long-term process, and should be prepared from the outset to stay the course.

- *Accountability.* Mutual accountability between donors and beneficiaries is essential to effective aid relationships. The ultimate beneficiaries of aid should be those whose rights are in jeopardy and who need better protection. More generally, they are the people served by the institutions that receive aid. In the final analysis, aid should be judged in relation to this objective, and governments, other national institutions and donors should measure their performance primarily against this test of accountability.

In addition, both donors and beneficiaries should ground the reform process and assistance efforts in international human rights standards.

Beneficiaries said that donors are more likely to achieve successful results where they recognise:

- *Flexibility and ability to evolve.* Donors should not be overly bureaucratic in their approval and reporting requirements, should respond quickly to changing local needs, and should devolve authority to local organisations as these acquire greater capacity.

If donors harmonised their use of terminology and reporting requirements, this would reduce the number of practical difficulties that beneficiaries face.

- *Build local ownership and capacity.* Wherever possible, donors should employ more local staff and use fewer foreign consultants. Tied aid should be avoided. Project funds should be spent locally. Projects should aim to increase the autonomy of local institutions and organisations.

- *Balance aid.* Successful reforms in the justice sector require both material and intellectual support. Aid providers should seek an appropriate balance between the two.

- *Show expertise and professionalism.* Many donors do not have staff who are knowledgeable in the fields of justice reform, international human rights standards or project management. Improved training would be helpful. Many organisations do not research adequately, or plan and consult sufficiently, before launching their programmes. Many improvements could be made if programmes were implemented with more forethought.

- *Respect local priorities and avoid imported solutions.* The objectives and priorities of justice reform should be determined locally. When donors compete, impose external priorities, follow "fads", or mix aid with other foreign policy objectives, they can slow or undermine the reform process.

- *Invest for the long-term.* Donors should avoid rigid "exit strategies", and the use of short-term indicators of success. Justice reform is a long-term process. In justice reform, sustainability cannot be measured in the short-term or solely in relation to the finances of local institutions and organisations.

- *Local presence.* Where those who provide aid are present locally, it is easier to ensure due attention to many of the factors listed above, including transparency, attention to local priorities, accountability and flexibility.

- *Use of intermediaries.* In many cases, particularly where they cannot be present locally, donor agencies should consider channelling assistance through intermediary organisations present in the country, such as foundations, NGO consortia, or local offices of intergovernmental organisations (such as the UN). Provided these intermediary organisations pay due regard to transparency and local participation, they are generally better equipped to ensure that foreign assistance enhances domestic ownership and provides effective and sustainable support for reform programmes.

ANNEXE I: **LIST OF PRINCIPAL INTERVIEWS**

In Cambodia, interviews were held with representatives of the following institutions:

Asian Development Bank; Ausaid, Criminal Justice Assistance Project (CJAP); Australian Embassy; Cambodian Bar Association; Cambodian Centre for the Protection of Children's Rights; Cambodian Human Rights and Development Association (ADHOC); Cambodian Institute for Co-operation and Peace; Cambodian Institute of Human Rights; Cambodian League for the Promotion and Defence of Human Rights (LICADHO); Cambodian Womens Crisis Centre; Cham Khmer Islamic Minority Human Rights & Development Association; Commissioner of Police, (Phnom Penh); Danchurchaid; Director of Prisons, (Phnom Penh); Embassy of Canada; Embassy of France; Embassy of Sweden; European Union (EU); ForumSyd; Government Human Rights Committee & Advisor to the Prime Minister; Human Rights Action Committee; International Human Rights Law Groups (IHRLG): Cambodia Defenders Project; Khmer Institute for Democracy; Legal Aid of Cambodia; Ministry of Justice; National Assembly, Commission on Human Rights and Reception of Complaints; Office of the General Prosecutor, Phnom Penh Court of Appeal; Office of the UN High Commissioner for Human Rights (OHCHR); Oxfam (UK); Siem Reap Court; Ministry of Interior; Siem Reap Police; Siem Reap Prison; Silaka; The Asia Foundation; United Nations Development Programme (UNDP); United States Agency for International Development (USAID); Vietnamese Association; Vigilance; Women for Prosperity; Women's Media Centre of Cambodia; World Bank.

In Bulgaria, interviews were held with representatives of the following institutions:

Access Association; Access to Information Programme; Association for European Integration & Human Rights, Plovdiv; British Know-How Fund, UK; Bulgarian Helsinki Committee; Bulgarian Human Rights Centre; Bulgarian Institute for Legal Development; Bulgarian Lawyers for Human Rights; Bulgarian Police; Center for the Study of Democracy, Council of Europe (CoE); Central and Eastern European Law Initiative of the American Bar Association (US/ABA/CEELI); Chief Prosecutor's Office; Civil Society Development Fund; Creating Effective Grassroots Alternatives (CEGA); Democracy Network Programme; Dimitrina Petrova, Euro-Roma Rights Centre; Embassy of the Netherlands; European Union (EU); Human Rights Project; Inter-ethnic Initiative for Human Rights; International Centre for Minority Studies and Intercultural Relations; Journalists for Tolerance; Judges; Ministry of Interior; Ministry of Justice; Open Society Foundation; Open Society Institute; Parliament; Prison Administration; Roma Foundation, Plovdiv Roma District; Romani Baht Foundation; Supreme Court of Cassation; Tolerance Foundation; United Nations Development Programme (UNDP); United Nations High Commissioner for Refugees (UNHCR); United States Agency for International Development (USAID); United States Information Service (USIS); Women's Alliance for Democracy; World Bank.

In Guatemala, interviews were held with representatives of the following institutions:

Alliance against Impunity; Army of Guatemala; Canada (CIDA); Centre for Legal Action on Human Rights (CALDH): Head Office; Centre for Legal Action on Human Rights (CALDH): Indigenous Peoples Unit; Centre for Legal Action on Human Rights (CALDH): Legal Office; Centre for Legal Action on Human Rights (CALDH): Women's Project Unit; Commission on Strengthening of Justice; Congcoop; Defensoria Maya; Denmark (Danida, Prodeca); European Union (EC); Foreign Ministry; Guatemalan Bar Association; Guatemalan Institute of Penal Law; Institute of Training for Sustainable Development (IAPADES); Inter-American Development Bank (IDB); Judicial Modernisation Commission; Judicial Studies School; Justice Co-ordination Instancia; Mack Foundation; Ministerio Publico (Prosecutors); MINUGUA; Netherlands; Presidential Human Rights Commissioner; Project Consultancy Services (Donor Consortium); Soros Foundation Guatemala (SFG); Supreme Court; United Nations Development Programme (UNDP); United States Agency for International Development (USAID); World Bank (IBRD).

In South Africa, interviews were held with representatives of the following institutions:

Africa Affairs; Black Sash; British Council South Africa; Ceasefire; Centre for Applied Legal Studies (CALS); Centre for the Study of Violence and Reconciliation; Constitutional Court; Danida; Department of Correctional Services; Department of Justice; EU Foundation; Freedom of Expression Institute; Human Rights Committee; Human Rights Institute of South Africa (HURISA); Independent Complaints Directorate; Institute for Democracy in South Africa (IDASA); Interfund; Justice College; Lawyers for Human Rights; Ministry of Foreign Affairs; National Paralegal Institute; National Prosecuting Authority; Office of the UN High Commissioner for Human Rights (OHCHR) Project Manager, South African Human Rights Commission (SAHRC); Office of the UN High Commissioner for Human Rights (OHCHR) Regional Office for Southern Africa; Penal Reform Project; Police Secretariat for Safety and Security; South African Human Rights Commission; South African National NGO Coalition (SANGOCO); South African Police Service, Human Rights Unit; United States Agency for International Development (USAID); Women in Law and Development (WILD); World Bank.

ANNEXE II: **LIST OF PERSONS WHO PROVIDED WRITTEN COMMENTS ON AN EARLIER VERSION OF THIS REPORT**

The International Council on Human Rights Policy would like to thank the following individuals and institutions for their comments on an earlier version of the present report.

Martin Abregu, Centre for Legal and Social Studies (CELS), Argentina.

Sadikou Ayo Alao, Founding Director, GERDDES AFRIQUE CIRD, Benin.

Iris Almeida, Director, Rights and Democracy, Montreal, Canada.

Heike Alefsen, Council of Europe, Strasbourg, France.

Richard Bourne, Director-designate, Commonwealth Policy Studies Unit, Institute of Commonwealth Studies, UK.

Bob Bradley, Cambodian Criminal Justice Assistance Project (AUSAID), Cambodia.

Marjolein Brouwer (and her colleagues), NOVIB, The Netherlands.

Sandra Colliver, Senior Rule of Law Adviser, International Foundation for Electoral Systems (IFES), Washington, USA.

Clarence J. Dias, International Center for Law in Development, New York, USA.

Robert Dossou, Director, Association pour la prévention de la délinquance juvénile (APDJ), Benin.

Anna Gavrilova-Ancheva, Executive Director, Bulgarian Lawyers for Human Rights, Bulgaria.

Henriette Geiger, Guatemala Office of the European Commission, Guatemala.

Yash Ghai, Sir Y. K. Pao Professor of Public Law, Hong Kong.

Annabelle Grant (and her colleagues), UK Department for International Development, London, UK.

Steve Golub, Boalt Hall School of Law, USA.

Thomas Hammarberg, Ambassador, Sweden.

Wolfgang Heinz, Free University, Berlin, Germany.

Peter Helmers, Office of the UN High Commissioner for Human Rights, Geneva, Switzerland.

Kaarina Immonen, Assistant Resident Representative, UNDP, Cambodia.

Bongani I. Khumalo, Director, Community Law and Rural Development Centre, Durban, South Africa.

John Lobsinger (and his colleagues), CIDA, Canada.

Francesca Marotta, Office of the UN High Commissioner for Human Rights, Geneva, Switzerland.

Ivaylo Maznev and Teodara Krumova, Lawyers, Bulgaria.

Nicholas Marcoux, Director, European Union Foundation for Human Rights in South Africa.

Amin Mekki Medani, Chief Technical Adviser, OHCHR, Gaza.

Richard E. Messick, World Bank, USA.

Valentin Mitev, Executive Director, Civil Society Development Foundation, Bulgaria.

Mary Ndlovu, Curriculum Co-ordinator, Legal Resources Foundation, Zimbabwe.

Koy Neam, Asia Foundation, Cambodia.

Thomas O'Brien, World Bank, USA.

Chidi Ansolm Odinkalu, Interights, London, UK.

Dr. Philista Onyango, African Network for the Prevention of and Protection against Child Abuse and Neglect, Regional Office, Kenya.

Sonny Ostberg, Field Director, ForumSyd, Cambodia.

Karin Poulsen and Victor Hugo Madrigal-Borloz, Danish Centre for Human Rights, Denmark.

Christophe Peschoux, Office of the UN High Commissioner for Human Rights, Geneva, Switzerland.

Borislav Petranov, Interights, London, UK.

Arend Pieper, Charge dAffaires, Netherlands Embassy, Guatemala.

James Ross, The Netherlands.

Dr Aboubacar Abdullah Senghore, African Centre for Democracy and Human Rights Studios, Gambia

Sigrun I. Skogly, Lancaster University, UK.

Myo Thant, Asian Development Bank, Cambodia.

Sophia Woodman, Research Director, Human Rights in China, Hong Kong.

ANNEXE III: **AN OVERVIEW OF DONOR POLICIES AND PROGRAMMES**

This annexe provides an overview of donor policies and programmes dealing with human rights assistance. It takes a broad-brush approach – highlighting the main donors and assistance providers, key policy statements and key areas of assistance.

The DAC

The Development Assistance Committee (DAC) of the Organisation for Economic Co-operation and Development (OECD) brings together official government aid agencies from the developed world (including the World Bank and the European Union). Private aid agencies also participate in its deliberations. Founded in 1961, the DAC is intended to (*inter alia*) "stimulate and harmonise its Members' efforts in favour of developing countries". As the principal OECD body charged with development related activities, DAC's mission is to "foster co-ordinated, integrated, effective and adequately financed international efforts in support of sustainable economic and social development".[28] The DAC first directly confronted the issues of democracy and governance in 1989,[29] when it declared that "the participatory development notion addresses both economic and political aspects of broad popular participation in the development process.... Participatory development implies more democracy, a greater role for local organisations and self-government, respect of human rights including effective and accessible legal systems...". [30] That statement would be followed by official pronouncements on human rights, democracy and development by the EU and a number of DAC countries in 1991, and by the introduction of the issue in several Consultative Group meetings thereafter.[31] The subsequent establishment of the DAC's "working party on participatory development and good governance" represents the DAC's adoption of this theme as a "major ongoing orientation of the Committee".[32]

A 1995 DAC policy statement identified six "key elements" of strategies for sustainable development.[33] Among these was "good governance and public management, democratic accountability, the protection of human rights and the

---

[28] See Development Assistance Committee of the OECD, *How the OECD's Development Assistance Committee Works*, at www.oecd.org/dac.

[29] See Helmut Fuhrer, *The Story of Official Development Assistance: A History of the Development Assistance Committee and the Development Co-Operation Directorate in Dates, Names and Figures*, OECD, Paris, 1996, (Doc. No. OCDE/GD(94)67), (chapter entitled 1989: "Development Cooperation in the 1990s and New Emphasis on Participatory Development and Environment", page 51) at www.oecd.org/dac.

[30] *Id.* at page 52.

[31] *Id.*

[32] See *DAC Working Parties*, at www.oecd.org/dac.

rule of law".[34] As part of its mandate to provide "authoritative policy guidance" for its members in the conduct of their development co-operation programmes, the DAC has published official guidelines on the subject entitled *Participatory Development and Good Governance*.[35] DAC's *Shaping the 21st Century: the Contribution of Development Co-operation*, published in 1996, stated that: "Essential to attainment of [measurable development] goals are qualitative factors in the evolution of more stable, safe, participatory and just societies. These include capacity development for effective, democratic and accountable governance, the protection of human rights and respect for the rule of law."[36]

Official bilateral aid agencies

Australia

Australian assistance is provided principally through AUSAID, the country's official development assistance agency. In December 1998, the Australian Ministry of Foreign Affairs announced a new official framework for supporting human rights through aid. That statement establishes human rights as a "high priority" to be addressed through the complementary channels of aid and high level diplomacy, with human rights sanctions to be employed in "extreme cases". The policy further establishes that economic, social and cultural rights are to be equally ranked with civil and political rights; that specific rights are to be addressed in aid programmes; that programmes are to emphasise "durable capacity"; and that support is to be provided for "the practical and attainable". While pursuing consultation and co-operation with partner countries, Australian assistance also aims to involve close links with Australian human rights organisations and institutions. Under the heading "governance", AUSAID supports seven sub-sectors, including "economic and financial management", "public sector capacity building" and "civil and political rights".[37] AUSAID is especially active in supporting national human rights commissions, and in work in the Asia-Pacific region. The Australian aid categories also include "children's rights", and "electoral assistance".[38] Australia maintains a Human Rights Fund which provides support to local and Australian organisations and the Office of the UN High Commissioner for Human Rights. A Centre for Democratic Institutions

---

[33] See OECD/DAC, *Development Partnerships in the New Global Context*, Paris, 1995, at www.oecd.org/dac.

[34] *Id.*

[35] OECD/DAC, *Participatory Development and Good Governance*, Development Cooperation Guideline Series, Paris, 1995, at www.oecd.org/dac.

[36] OECD/DAC, *Shaping the 21st Century: the Contribution of Development Cooperation*, Paris, 1996, (*Introduction: values and interests*), at www.oecd.org/dac.

[37] To which the agency's budget committed 148 million Australian dollars for the 1999-2000 biennium. See *AUSAID, Governance*, www.ausaid.gov.au.

[38] For example, AUSAID committed from 10 to 15 million Australian dollars for the 1999 elections in Indonesia. *Id.*

was established in 1998 to provide further support in this area.

Austria

Austria's Federal Ministry of Foreign Affairs states that the objective of Austrian development co-operation is to promote sustainable economic development in partner countries. To these ends, "[t]he principles of respect for human rights, promotion of democratic institutions and good governance, gender equality and environmental protection form the basis of the Austrian Development Co-operation". Austria's official development policy requires that "these principles be taken into account in all programmes and projects".[39] The Austrian Federal Ministry of Foreign Affairs also advocates strong international assistance for strengthening of the rule of law, as part of its traditional foreign policy emphasis on peace building. In 1998, it was host to an international conference on justice reform and development and establishing the rule of law in post-conflict situations. During that conference, the Austrian State Secretary for Foreign Affairs emphasised the need to "redouble… efforts… to strengthen… the implementation of international human rights standards at the national level". In an important statement of policy, the Secretary declared that "international assistance is vital and often an important incentive towards the consolidation of peace", requiring that "such assistance must be [made more] targeted and co-ordinated".[40]

Belgium

While a review of recent reports suggests that rule of law or justice sector assistance do not feature prominently in Belgian development co-operation, the country has sought to integrate human rights into its programming. The Belgian Foreign Ministry lists three main areas of emphasis in its development co-operation policy, including "(1) attention for human rights, democratisation and good governance; (2) building partnerships; (3) combating poverty by dealing with 'dualism' (a world divided into rich and poor)". Recognising that the universality and indivisibility of human rights are elements of Belgian development policy, the Ministry maintains that "[...]the political emancipation process must run parallel to economic and social protection" and that "[f]reedom and justice go hand in hand with well-being and welfare".[41]

Canada

Through the Canadian International Development Agency (CIDA), Canada has been among the most active donors in supporting rule of law development, and in seeking to integrate human rights into its development activities. Official CIDA

---

[39] See *Austrian Development Cooperation*, www.bmaa.gv.at.

[40] See Benita Ferrero-Waldner, Austrian State Secretary for Foreign Affairs, Opening Speech, Austrian Federal Ministry of Foreign Affairs, *Building Justice: A Conference Commemorating the Fifth Anniversary of the World Conference on Human Rights*, Vienna, 1998, at page 32.

[41] See *Belgian Development Cooperation*, www.diplobel.fgov.be.

literature lists three key objectives of Canadian foreign policy: the promotion of prosperity and employment; the protection of (Canadian) security, within a stable global framework; and the projection of Canadian values and culture. Among the "Canadian values" to be projected, Canada lists "respect for human rights, democracy, the rule of law...". Canadian development assistance itself has six express priorities, one of which is "human rights, democracy, and good governance".[42] Human rights thus "are, and will continue to be a priority for Canada's international assistance programmes", according to CIDA and the Department of Foreign Affairs and International Trade.[43]

Denmark

Through DANIDA (Danish International Development Agency) Denmark too has been very active in providing human rights assistance. Danish development policy, set out in its new policy framework document *Partnership 2000*, includes extensive reference to human rights. The Danish Minister for Development Co-operation notes that the most important principles of Danish development policy include fighting poverty, promoting the environment, involving both men and women in development, and strengthening democracy and respect for human rights.[44] Denmark views human rights as a "cross-cutting" issue in development assistance, and spent roughly 1.7 billion DKK on related programmes in the 1990-98 period. DANIDA recently completed a comprehensive evaluation of its support to the promotion of human rights and democratisation, which noted that Danish bilateral assistance for these areas has expanded rapidly during the 1990s.[45]

Finland

Finland's foreign and development policy, as implemented through the Foreign Ministry and the Finnish Department for International Development Co-operation, is linked by human rights objectives; development co-operation is expressly identified as a tool of human rights policy. According to that policy "human rights, equality, democracy and good governance constitute one of the main aims of development co-operation".[46]

---

[42] See Canadian Development Assistance, www.acdi-cida.gc.ca

[43] Id.

[44] See *Partnership 2000: Danish Overseas Development Assistance*, www.um.dk.

[45] See DANIDA, *Evaluation of Danish Support to Promotion of Human Rights and Democratization*, Synthesis Report, (March 2000), www.evaluation.dk

[46] See *Human Rights and Finland's Foreign Policy: Report by Foreign Minister Tarja Halonen to the Foreign Affairs Committee of Parliament on the Human Rights Policy of the Finnish Government*, November 11 1998, available at www.virtual.finland.fi. See also www.global.finland.fi.

France

Official French development policy has five express priority aims: supporting economic independence and integration in the global economy; strengthening government institutions and the foundations of democracy; fighting poverty and providing social services; improving research opportunities and access to scientific information; and continuing regional co-operation and integration processes. Under the second priority area (government and democracy), France includes public administration, the judiciary, democracy and human rights. While neither justice nor the rule of law are sectors as such in the French development assistance framework, elements thereof are subsumed under other sectors, and France has been especially active in providing legal assistance in francophone countries.[47]

Germany

German development aid in these areas is implemented principally through the official agencies "GTZ"[48] and "BMZ".[49] Among the 15 thematic and project areas of GTZ is the category "Economic and Social Policy, Law and Administration". This is itself sub-divided into a number of areas, among them "Law" (legislative development, legal stability, legal enforcement, democracy and liberty, including support for judicial reform, and "human rights questions") and "Institutional Reforms and Public Administration".[50] BMZ refers to a single aim of German development policy: improve living conditions, particularly for the poorest, through sustainable development. For this, BMZ sees 3 pre-requisites: productive economic growth, social justice and ecological sustainability. The three express priority areas of BMZ assistance are poverty alleviation, environmental protection and education and training. For BMZ (and the German Government) human rights feature not only as a development assistance area, but especially as criteria for receiving German assistance. Specifically, "criteria for the deployment of instruments and funds... are as follows: respect for human rights; popular participation in political decisions; the rule of law and the certainty of the law...." If a basic threshold is met, BMZ will help a partner country to improve performance in these areas through assistance, and improvements will lead to higher levels of assistance.[51]

---

[47] See www.france.diplomatie.fr.

[48] *Deutsche Gesellschaft für Technische Zusammenarbeit*. See www.gtz.de.

[49] *Bundesministerium für wirtschaftliche Zusammenbarbeit und Entwicklung*. See www.bmz.de.

[50] See www.gtz.de.

[51] See www.bmz.de.

Ireland

Ireland has established a human rights unit within the Ministry of Foreign Affairs, earmarked separate programmes and budget lines for human rights assistance, and "attache[d] priority to human rights in terms of Ireland's foreign policy".[52] Ireland Aid, the Development Co-operation Division of the Department of Foreign Affairs, "has a special focus on the fostering of human rights and democracy". According to the agency, Ireland supports human rights and democratisation projects in a many countries. These projects include activities such as grass roots human rights and democracy education programmes, election monitoring and support for the development of parliamentary and judicial structures.

Italy

Italy, through its Ministry of Foreign Affairs, extends direct forms of assistance to selected countries, especially those among the country's Balkan neighbours. Italy has been an important provider of support for democratisation and reform in Central America. In addition, the country is a significant supporter of multilateral human rights assistance programmes such as those of the UN and the EU.

Japan

Japan provides assistance for legal reform and democracy through its Ministry of Foreign Affairs[53], the Japan International Co-operation Agency (JICA)[54] and the Japan Bank for International Co-operation (JBIC).[55] Japan is today one of the largest contributors, in financial terms, of development assistance for human rights, democracy, rule of law and good governance. In its official policy, the Japanese Ministry of Foreign Affairs states that "strengthening the foundations of democracy promotes the participation of people in governance and development and leads to the protection and promotion of human rights, so it is an extremely important factor in promoting... stability and development".[56] Japan's "ODA Charter"[57] stipulates that "full attention should be paid to efforts for promoting democratisation...[and] the securing of basic human rights and freedoms in the recipient country". To these ends, Japan (principally through JICA) provides support for "the establishment of functional legal, administrative, and police systems, which are the foundations of a democratic system". The country has supported justice system reform in a wide range of countries, including Vietnam and Cambodia, sponsored democratisation initiatives in Africa, Asia and Latin

[52] See *Irish Official Development Assistance*, www.irlgov.ie

[53] See www.mofa.go.jp.

[54] See www.jica.go.jp.

[55] See www.jbic.go.jp.

[56] See Government of Japan, Ministry of Foreign Affairs, *Japan's Support for Democratization*, September 1999, at www.mofa.go.jp.

[57] See *Japan's ODA Charter*, Government of Japan, Cabinet Decisions, June 30, 1992, at www.mofa.go.jp.

America, and funded electoral support in Cambodia, Bosnia, Nigeria, Central African Republic, Guinea, Lesotho and Ecuador.

Netherlands

Official Netherlands policy on human rights and development co-operation is summarised in the document Dutch Policy on Human Rights.58 The government states that "Dutch foreign policy... expresses a strong national commitment to human rights", and recognises that "development co-operation can... be used to promote human rights. Aid can be deployed to encourage and support compliance with human rights agreements and democratisation in developing countries". The Dutch Foreign Ministry does this through "efforts to strengthen the institutional framework and the training of members of the judiciary and public prosecutors [...] fostering democracy,... and supporting government efforts in the field of [human] rights". Among the six aims of Dutch development policy is support for "good governance". In 1996 alone, Dutch spending on human rights and democratisation was estimated to be 398 million NLG (over $160 million).

New Zealand

A "strong commitment to human rights" is cited by New Zealand as the basis for the country's policy to "increasingly... assist... bilaterally with human rights capacity building". The government does so usually through NZODA (New Zealand Official Development Agency) including through the agency's designated Good Governance Fund. This is a focus area for NZODA,[59] and, reflecting this prioritisation, the agency's 1999/2000 budget includes expanded provision for "law and justice capacity building", with a particular focus on the South Pacific region.[60]

Norway

Human rights assistance and human rights principles are featured throughout Norway's official development policy framework.[61] Active in human rights assistance throughout the 1990s, Norway expected in 1999 to expand human rights assistance interventions through NORAD (Norwegian Agency for Development Co-operation), NORDEM (Norwegian Resource Bank for Democracy and Human Rights), and the Ministry of Foreign Affairs.[62] The Norwegian Minister of International Development and Human Rights announced

---

[58] Ministry of Foreign Affairs of the Netherlands, *Dutch Policy on Human Rights*, at www.bz.minbuza.nl

[59] See NZODA, *Good Governance: Investing in a Common Future*, at www.mft.govt.nz.

[60] See the description of the New Zealand Ministry of Foreign Affairs and Trade and NZODA policy contained in *New Zealand and the International Community: Human Rights*, at www.mft.govt.nz. New Zealand also supports the UN's Voluntary Fund for Technical Cooperation in the Field of Human Rights. *Id.*

[61] See, e.g., Government of Norway, *Report to the Storting: A Changing World—Main Elements of Norwegian Policy Towards Developing Countries*, no. 19 (1995-96), at www.odin.dep.no.

in October 1999 that "Norway...intends to increase our assistance to legal and electoral systems, the rule of law, and building expertise in civil society and human rights organisations".[63]

Portugal

Portugal's "co-operation for development" programme focuses principally on Portuguese speaking African countries and aims to "promote improved living conditions in developing countries and to consolidate democracy and the rule of law". [64] Portugal now emphasises two areas of development co-operation: (1) private sector development; and (2) "strengthening the governance systems of ...the Portuguese speaking countries in Africa, focusing particularly on legal systems and the judiciary, but also extending to parliamentary institutions, electoral systems, local governments and constitutional advice".[65]

Spain

AECI (*Agencia Española De Cooperación Internacional*), Spain's official development co-operation agency, is particularly active in Latin America, the Mediterranean, the Arab world, the Philippines, and a small group of sub-Saharan African nations. AECI lists among its principal objectives the strengthening of democratic institutions. Especially in Latin America, a broad range of assistance is provided in relation to governance, democratisation, and rule of law development. This includes support to justice systems, elections, police reform, and penal systems.[66]

Sweden

SIDA (the Swedish International Development Agency) describes international development co-operation as an investment (*inter alia*) in "democracy and equality". The six official goals of the programme include "democratic development", "social equality", and "gender equality". SIDA supports democratic development because it "considers that the fulfilment of certain minimum requirements is necessary for democratic governance: free elections..., an independent legal system and fundamental democratic rights and privileges".[67] In the field of human rights, much of SIDA's work is implemented through 14 Swedish "framework organisations". These are Swedish-based church groups, solidarity organisations, non-governmental aid agencies, and unions, among

[62] See www.odin.dep.no.

[63] See Norwegian Minister of International Development and Human Rights Hilde F. Johnson, address to the Council of Europe, *Toward a New Human Rights Agenda*, 16 October 1999, at www.odin.dep.no.

[64] See Government of Portugal, Ministry of Foreign Affairs, *Cooperation for Development*, at www.min-nestrangeiros.pt.

[65] Government of Portugal, Ministry of Foreign Affairs, *DAC Aid Review of Portugal*, (press release, June 1997), at www.min-nestrangeiros.pt.

[66] See Government of Spain, AECI, at www.aeci.es.

them Diakonia,[68] Swedish Save the Children,[69] and ForumSyd.[70]

Switzerland

Swiss policy on development co-operation is based on four basic principles, one of which is the maintenance of peace and security and the promotion of human rights, democracy and the principles of the rule of law.[71] Switzerland seeks to achieve this by supporting a range of relevant governmental and non-governmental institutions, including human rights groups and justice sector institutions. In South Africa, for example, SDC (Swiss Agency for Development and Co-operation) supports "good governance" and "democratic institutions", as well as providing direct support to South African NGOs.[72] A resolution adopted by the Swiss Federal Council in 1999 linked Swiss development assistance to Swiss foreign policy action, and established criteria for enhancing or withdrawing aid, and made reference to respect for human rights.[73]

United Kingdom

The United Kingdom, through DFID (the Department for International Development), the Foreign and Commonwealth Office and the British Know How Fund[74], is among the most visible of bilateral donors in the field of human rights assistance. The Government's development policy is set out in a White Paper *Eliminating World Poverty: A Challenge for the 21st Century*, which specifically pledges attention to human rights in British foreign aid. According to that policy document, the government will: "Give particular attention to human rights, transparent and accountable government and core labour standards...".[75] The paper recognises that: "The State must also provide a framework of law and regulation within which people can exercise their rights.... Sustainable development is not possible unless human rights are protected for all...". British development assistance is to support "good governance and the rule of law".

In addition, the UK has officially committed itself to the adoption of a rights-based

---

[67] See www.sida.se.

[68] See www.diakonia.se.

[69] See www.rb.se.

[70] See www.forumsyd.se.

[71] The others relate to increasing prosperity, promoting social cohesion, and preserving the environment. See Swiss Agency for Development and Cooperation at www.sdc-gov.ch.

[72] See www.sdc-gov.ch.

[73] The resolution was adopted on 20 September 1999. See SDC, *Political Conditionality: Improving Coherence*, in News in Brief from the SDC (Newsletter No. 6, December 1999) at www.sdc-gov.ch.

[74] The British Know How Fund is Britain's programme of assistance to countries of Central and Eastern Europe and Central Asia, supporting work on human rights, police reform, judicial reform, etc. www.dfid.gov.uk.

approach to development.[76] In its annual human rights report for 1999, the government defined this approach as one which "means making people the central purpose of development... by allowing them to speak for themselves". The report explains that "this differs from the old approach to development where the needs of developing country populations were too often defined by government officials or international institutions without consultation with the people on whose behalf they claimed to act".[77] At the same time, promoting the rule of law and fair justice administration are set out as key UK foreign policy and development objectives. The report announces a new approach to assistance to the legal sector, which includes support for the sector as a whole, as well as to individual institutions such as police, courts and prisons, and to non-formal systems. New attention is to be paid to public safety and security, as well as to improved access.[78] The UK's New Models of Accessible Justice and Penal Reform Project,[79] is designed to develop new approaches to supporting traditional and alternative dispute resolution options, non-custodial measures, reforming prisons, strengthening juvenile justice, and guarantees against discrimination in legal systems. Finally, the UK Foreign and Commonwealth Office also provides a Human Rights Project Fund, financing a broad range of human rights development activities, including "rule of law co-operation", "prison reform", "combating torture", and "promoting the rights of vulnerable groups".[80]

United States of America

The United States Agency for International Development (USAID), the official development agency, has had some involvement in human rights assistance programmes for many years, but it was only in the 1990's that USAID's activities in this field became a normal part of its programmes.[81] Today, according to USAID, "expanding the global community of democracies is a key objective of U.S. foreign policy".

USAID has identified four "democracy sectors": rule of law, elections, civil society, and governance. Based upon an official US national security strategy,[82] USAID's 1997 "strategic plan" sets out four objectives for these programmes: "[strengthening] rule of law and respect for human rights of women [and] men;

[75] See *Eliminating World Poverty: A Challenge for the 21st Century*, section 3 paragraph 7, at www.dfid.gov.uk.

[76] See *White Paper on International Development*, November 1997, at www.dfid.gov.uk.

[77] UK Foreign and Commonwealth Office and Department for International Development, *Annual Report for 1999, Human Rights*, July 1999, Chapter 2, page 17, (*A Rights Based Approach to Development*) at www.hrpd.fco.gov.uk.

[78] *Id.*, at Chapter 5, pages 46-57, (*Rights and Justice*).

[79] This is a global project with six pilot countries in Africa, Asia and the Caribbean. See www.dfid.gov.uk.

[80] See www.hrpd.fco.gov.uk.

[encouraging] credible and competitive political processes; [encouraging] the development of politically active civil society; [encouraging] more transparent and accountable government institutions".[83] The agency established a Center for Democracy and Governance in May of 1994, to support its programming in these areas, and maintains a separate programme to administer democracy projects. Based up on its experience (both successes and failures) with such programmes, and following a series of evaluations, USAID has introduced a conceptual framework for democracy and governance programming;[84] developed a Handbook of Democracy and Governance Programme Indicators; and published a detailed manual on developing rule of law programmes.[85]

European Union

The official objective of European Union (EU) development co-operation is to "foster sustainable development designed to eradicate poverty in developing countries and to integrate them into the world economy". This is to be achieved in part by "pursuing policies that promote the consolidation of democracy, the rule of law, good governance, and respect for human rights".[86] In June of 1991, the EU adopted a policy statement on human rights, which was to serve as the principal reference for the organisation throughout the decade.[87] The European Council Declaration on Human Rights identified the protection of human rights as "one of the cornerstones of European co-operation",[88] and held that democracy, pluralism and respect for human rights are "essential prerequisites of sustained economic and social development". The EU and its members were thus to use development co-operation agreements to promote human rights within third countries.

Subsequently, the Council adopted a second resolution, detailing means by which assistance programmes provided by the EU and EU member states might help to

[81] See USAID, *History of USAID Democracy and Governance Activities*, at www.info.usaid.gov.

[82] See U.S. Government, The White House, *A National Security Strategy of Engagement and Enlargement* (Washington DC: U.S. Government Printing Office, 1996) at www.info.usaid.gov.

[83] See *USAID's Strategic Plan*, www.info.usaid.gov.

[84] See USAID, *Democracy and Governance: A Conceptual Framework*, November 1998, at www.info.usaid.gov.

[85] See USAID, *Weighing in on the Scales of Justice: Strategic Approaches for Donor-supported Rule of Law Programmes*, Feb. 1994, at www.info.usaid.gov.

[86] See European Union, *EC Development Cooperation Mission Statement* at www.europa.eu.int.

[87] EU, *European Council Declaration on Human Rights*, Luxembourg, June 1991. This followed a less elaborated declaration on human rights of the Community's Foreign Ministers adopted on 21 July 1986.

[88] *Id.*, at paragraph 1.

achieve those ends.[89] In that resolution, a pledge was made to increase development co-operation and other forms of support for human rights, good governance, democracy and the rule of law in developing countries, and to integrate those themes throughout future co-operation programmes. During the 1990s, the European Union became ever more involved as a provider of assistance for human rights, democracy, and the rule of law in developing countries and post-Soviet European states. Programmes at various levels include the European Initiative for Democracy and the Protection of Human Rights; various development agreements under the Lomé IV Convention;[90] and a number of special programmes, including PHARE, MEDA, and TACIS.[91] The Development Directorate-General of the European Union (Commission) is responsible for development assistance to what are referred to in EU language as 20 "OCTs" (overseas countries and territories) and 71 "ACP countries" (African, Caribbean and Pacific States).[92]

International financial institutions

The World Bank is a relatively recent addition to the list of international providers of assistance for good governance and legal and judicial reform. It is, as well, still careful in its express engagement in matters of human rights.[93] Nevertheless, the Bank has emerged as a leading actor in this field. Today, support for "good governance" is a common element of World Bank programmes, albeit largely with an approach geared to strengthening national policies and institutions necessary to underpin economic reforms and private investment.[94] This includes support for legal and judicial development and reform, and the Bank is actively engaged in supporting such activities in countries across the globe. It maintains a web page on law and development,[95] through which a new Bank database on legal and judicial reform (including judicial system performance indicators) can be accessed.

---

[89] EU, *Resolution of the Council and of the Member States Meeting in the Council on Human Rights, Democracy and Development*, Brussels, 28 November 1991.

[90] See the Fourth Lomé Convention, as revised by Agreement in Mauritius on 4 November 1995, at article 5 and article 224(m).

[91] See European Commission, *The European Union's PHARE and TACIS Democracy Programme: Compendium of Ad-hoc Projects 1993-1997* (1998); see also *Evaluation of the PHARE and TACIS Democracy Programme1992-1997*, at www.europa.eu.int/comm/dg1a/evaluation/ptdp, and; European Commission, *Democratization, the Rule of Law, Respect for Human Rights and Good Governance: the Challenges of the Partnership between the European Union and the ACP States*, (Doc. No. COM (1998) 146 final, 12.03.1998).

[92] See generally, EU, European Commission, *Commission Communication to the Parliament: Democratization, the rule of law, respect for human rights and good governance: the challenges of the partnership between the European Union and the ACP States*, 12 March 1998 (COM(98)146).

In 1998, the Bank also published a booklet on its approach to the issue of human rights and development, in which it recognised that "creating the conditions for the attainment of human rights is a central and irreducible goal of development".[96] The Bank's position, as articulated in that document, now recognises its responsibility in ensuring that human rights are fully respected in connection with the projects it supports; underscores its direct role in contributing to economic and social rights through development loans and assistance; and takes into account an important if indirect role for the Bank in contributing to the realisation of civil and political rights through support for good governance, strong judicial systems and other requirements of an enabling environment for rights protection.

Since the early 1990's, the regional development banks, including the Inter-American Development Bank (IDB), the Asian Development Bank (ADB), the European Bank for Reconstruction and Development (EBRD),[97] and (to a lesser degree) the African Development Bank (AfDB),[98] have also variously supported efforts at improving governance and legal development. For example, the Asian Development Bank is an active donor in the legal and judicial development field in Cambodia,[99] and, in 1998, the Inter-American Development Bank approved a $25 million loan for justice reform in Guatemala. While showing some reticence in the direct use of the term "governance" in its policies and

---

[93] Especially prior to the 1990s, the World Bank, based upon a restrictive interpretation of its own charter (limiting it to economic considerations and prohibiting political involvement), expressly ruled out any direct involvement in human rights projects and abstained from considering human rights aspects of Bank projects or the human rights performance of its national partners. While Bank activity in areas of governance has increased dramatically, this remains an important factor in the Bank's profile today. The Bank's reticence in this area is a much debated subject. See, for example, *The World Bank, Development and Human Rights: the Role of the World Bank*, Washington, September 1998, at page 3; The World Bank, *Governance and Development*, Washington, April 1992, at page 50; Patricia Feeney, *Accountable Aid: Local Participation in Major Projects*, Oxfam, UK 1998; Katarina Tomasevski, *Development Aid and Human Rights*, New York, 1989, at pages 30-36; Lawyers Committee for Human Rights and The Institute for Policy Research and Advocacy, *In the Name of Development*, New York, 1995, at page 54; Lawyers Committee for Human Rights and the Venezuelan Program for Human Rights Education and Action, *Halfway to Reform: The World Bank and the Venezuelan Justice System*, New York, 1996, at page 25.

[94] See *World Bank Programmes*, at www.worldbank.org.

[95] www1.worldbank.org/legal.

[96] The World Bank, *Development and Human Rights: the Role of the World Bank*, Washington, September 1998, at page 2.

[97] The EBRD is exceptional in that its charter includes a provision conditioning assistance on democracy. See Agreement Establishing the European Bank for Reconstruction and Development, Art. 1, (May 1990), and the discussion in Lawyers Committee for Human Rights and The Institute for Policy research and Advocacy, *In the Name of Development*, New York, 1995, at page 13.

programmes (often using the substitution "institutional development"), the African Development Bank began to examine these issues in the mid-1990s.[100]

The United Nations

The UN is one of the oldest providers of human rights assistance, and, in particular, of assistance to the justice sector. Rule of law and justice sector assistance (dating back to the 1950s) has been principally delivered through the UN programme of advisory services and technical assistance in the field of human rights, a programme implemented by the Office of the High Commissioner for Human Rights (OHCHR) and its predecessor institutions.[101] Other UN agencies and programmes too are involved in these areas, most notably the United Nations Development Programme (UNDP), the International Labour Organisation (ILO) (labour laws and dispute resolution mechanisms), UNICEF (child rights and juvenile justice development), UNESCO (human rights in education), DPKO (the Department of Peacekeeping Operations) (justice reform in conflict and post conflict countries), and the Centre for International Crime Prevention (CICP) (criminal justice reforms), and others.[102] A UN system-wide analysis of human rights assistance programmes found that the amount of such assistance available within the UN system was "significant".

The OHCHR administered *United Nations Programme of Advisory Services and Technical Assistance in the Field of Human Rights* has focused principally on the strengthening of the rule of law[103] through assistance for constitutional and legislative reform and support for lawyers, judges, prosecutors, police, prisons, parliaments, NGOs, national human rights commissions, and other key actors and institutions. A small programme of limited significance for most of the first forty years of its operation, the programme underwent a dramatic period of growth between 1987 and 1997.[104] Today, the programme is active in rule of law

---

[98] For a useful review of the Asian and African Development Bank's evolving approach to governance, see Morten Boas, *Governance as Multilateral Development Bank Policy: The Cases of the African Development Bank and the Asian Development Bank, in Development and Rights: Negotiating Justice in Changing Societies* (Christian Lund, ed.), London, 1999, at pages 117-134.

[99] See Remarks of Richard Eyre, Assistant General Counsel of the Asian Development Bank, in Government of Cambodia and UNDP, *International Conference on Cambodian Legal Reform in the Context of Sustainable Development* (Sok Siphana, ed.), Cambodian Legal Resources Development Centre, Phnom Penh, 1998, at page 37.

[100] See African Development Bank, *The Democratization Process in Africa, Governance and the Role of the African Development Bank: Recommendations of the African Development Bank Advisory Council*, Abidjan, 1994.

[101] The predecessor of OHCHR was the UN Centre for Human Rights, which was itself preceded by the UN Division for Human Rights.

[102] See United Nations, Office of the High Commissioner for Human Rights, *System Wide Analysis of United Nations Technical Cooperation Activities in Human Rights Related Areas*, Geneva, 1999 (unnumbered doc.).

development and justice reforms in several countries in Africa, Asia, the Middle East, Latin America and Central and Eastern Europe.

UNDP, the UN system's largest development co-operation programme, has itself become increasingly involved in justice sector development and in human rights assistance since the early 1990s. Judged by the number and size of projects, UNDP was the largest UN provider of such assistance by the end of the decade.[105] The programme's adoption in January 1998 of a new policy document entitled *Integrating Human Rights with Sustainable Human Development*[106] marked the consolidation of an internal policy review process on the place of human rights in development programming. By the end of 1999, UNDP had human rights assistance projects under way in all regions of the world, including justice sector projects in at least twenty-four countries. Various democracy and governance programmes were being carried out in several countries, including activities directed at strengthening national human rights commissions; national plans of action; parliaments; electoral systems; courts; police; prisons; NGOs; and a host of other relevant institutions.[107]

[103]The rule of law focus came as a result of the historical application of the programme mandate. The resolution establishing the programme (Id.) required that the kinds of assistance provided be determined by the particular requests received. (Id. at para. 3 (a)). As most requests related to rule of law institutions, these are the capacities that the programme developed related to those areas. What is more, the establishing resolution expressly excluded activities "for which adequate advisory services [are] available through a specialized agency" as well as those areas which fell "within the scope of existing technical assistance programmes." (Id.). As rule of law assistance was not elsewhere available in the UN system, (while programmes related to health, education, housing, etc. were) the advisory services programme focused its work in this area.

[104]For an overview of these developments, and the history of the programme, see Mokhiber, Craig, "The United Nations Programme of Technical Cooperation in the Field of Human Rights", in *Human Rights Monitoring Procedures: A Textbook on Petitioning and Lobbying International Organizations*, (Raoul Wallenberg Institute of Human Rights and Humanitarian Law, 1996, forthcoming); see also, Benomar, Jamal, "Technical Cooperation in the Field of Human Rights, Past and Present, Reflections for Further Development", in *The Universal Declaration of Human Rights*, New York, 1998; and Rishmawi, Mona, "Human Rights in Development: UN Technical Cooperation in the Field of Human Rights", in *40th International Seminar for Diplomats: the Universal Protection of Human Rights: Translating International Commitments into National Action*, (Austrian Federal Ministry for Foreign Affairs, August 1997).

[105]See United Nations Development Programme, *Survey of UNDP Activities in Human Rights*, Management Development and Governance Division, August 1999, UNDP, New York.

[106]United Nations Development Programme, *Integrating Human Rights with Sustainable Human Development*, UNDP New York, 1998.[107] See United Nations Development Programme, *Survey of UNDP Activities in Human Rights*, Management Development and Governance Division, August 1999, UNDP, New York.

[107]See United Nations Development Programme, *Survey of UNDP Activities in Human Rights*, Management Development and Governance Division, August 1999, UNDP, New York.

The United Nations Development Assistance Framework (UNDAF) is being developed to respond to the challenge of co-ordinating aid programmes undertaken by different UN agencies. UNDAF is a "common programme and resources framework" for UN development agencies and programmes (in the first instance, members of the UN Development Group, and "whenever possible," other agencies of the UN system). It is intended to "maximise the developmental impact of UN assistance by the introduction of goal-oriented collaboration in response to national development priorities...". The UNDAF process in each country is to be based upon a Common Country Assessment (CCA), providing an overview of national development based upon a common set of indicators. The indicators are to reflect the priorities and mandates of UN organisations, as well as internationally agreed goals set by the various world conferences, including the 1993 World Conference on Human Rights. A Country Strategy Note (CSN), prepared by the Government with the participation and assistance of the UN system, is to complete the UNDAF package by establishing the national perspective and agreeing on how the United Nations system can contribute to the development objectives of each country. [108]

Private foundations and non-governmental donors

Human rights assistance generally, and justice sector support in particular, involves a vast array of non-governmental aid givers, alongside their official counterparts. Like official donors, private and non-governmental aid providers vary in their approach, strengths and weaknesses. Some function as implementers or funding channels for official donors, while others draw from their own endowments and pooled contributions to assist partners in developing countries. Most focus the bulk of their support on non-governmental beneficiaries and partners in beneficiary countries, while some are also involved in working with judges, police, prisons and other official sector beneficiaries. While some see themselves as donors and advisors in the traditional sense, others view their role as one of "solidarity" with domestic partners. Leading organisations in this category include Netherlands-based groups like NOVIB, ICCO and HIVOS; British based Oxfam; Danchurchaid based in Denmark, Norwegian People's Aid (Norway); and Diakonia, based in Sweden. Many of these groups are highly valued by beneficiaries for their commitment to partnership approaches, and to local participation and ownership. Some, like NOVIB, have pioneered rights-based approaches to assistance.

Among the most active of the private foundations in the justice sector, and in human rights assistance generally, are the Ford and Soros Foundations. The

[108]For further information see Office of the High Commissioner for Human Rights, *System Wide Analysis of United Nations Technical Cooperation Activities in Human Rights Related Areas*, Geneva, 1999 (unnumbered doc.), and UNDP, *Survey of UNDP Activities in Human Rights*, Management Development and Governance Division, August 1999, UNDP, New York.

mission statement of the Ford Foundation lists four goals: strengthen democratic values; reduce poverty and injustice; promote international co-operation; and advance human achievement. To these ends, Ford provides grants or loans to local institutions working in these areas. Under one of three designated programme areas, "Peace and Social Justice", funding is provided for organisations working on human rights and international co-operation, including "access to justice and protection of rights", and "governance and civil society" (public participation, accountable government, equality, and the rule of law).[109] Soros is a network of foundations and institutes, under the umbrella of the Soros Foundations Network. These include the Open Society Institute and national "open society foundations" across the former Soviet Union and Central and Eastern Europe, as well as in Guatemala, Haiti, South Africa and Mongolia.[110] It also funds the Constitutional and Legal Policy Institute (COLPI), to support legal reform efforts.[111] Soros works to establish "open societies" in its partner countries, and its foundations place a particular emphasis on local ownership and empowerment.

A number of legal and law based associations act variously as international advisors, aid providers, or implementers. The most visible among them are the Geneva-based International Commission of Jurists (ICJ) and its northern based affiliates (such as ICJ Sweden), Australian International Legal Resources (AILR), the International Human Rights Law Group (IHRLG), Interights, and the Central and Eastern European Law Initiative of the American Bar Association (CEELI). Such organisations often receive official donor funding (for example, from USAID, AUSAID, SIDA, or the EU) to implement projects in developing countries. Most think the technical and legal expertise they offer adds value to the assistance projects in which they participate.

[109]See Ford Foundation, Annual Report for 1998, available online at www.fordfound.org.

[110]See *The Soros Foundations Network* at www.soros.org.

[111]See the *Constitutional and Legal Policy Institute* at www.osi.hu/colpi.

BIBLIOGRAPHY

Further Reading

Adhoc, Licadho and Human Rights Watch, *Impunity in Cambodia: How Human Rights Offenders Escape Justice*, (Adhoc, Licadho and Human Rights Watch, Phnom Penh, June 1999).

African Development Bank, *The Democratization Process in Africa, Governance and the Role of the African Development Bank: Recommendations of the African Development Bank Advisory Council*, (ABD, Abidjan, 1994).

Agunga, Robert, *Talking it Out: A Communications-Based Approach to Sustainable Development*, (Harvard International Review, Winter 1998/1999, Vol. XXI, No.1, at pages 62-65).

Alston, Philip, *Human Rights Law*, (New York, New York University Press, 1996).

Anderson, Mary, *Do No Harm: How Aid Can Support Peace or War*, (Lynne Rienner, New York, 1999).

The Asia Foundation, *TAF Annual Report 1998*, (section entitled "Supporting Human Rights In Cambodia", TAF, Washington, 1999).

Austrian Federal Ministry of Foreign Affairs, *Building Justice: A Conference Commemorating the Fifth Anniversary of the World Conference on Human Rights*, (Vienna, 1998).

Benomar, Jamal, "Technical Cooperation in the Field of Human Rights, Past and Present, Reflections for Further Development", in *The Universal Declaration of Human Rights*, (UNDP, New York, 1998).

Biekart, Kees, *The Politics of Civil Society Building: European Private Aid Agencies and Democratic Transitions in Central America*, (International Books, Utrecht, 1999).

Boas, Morten, "Governance as Multilateral Development Bank Policy: The Cases of the African Development Bank and the Asian Development Bank", in *Development and Rights: Negotiating Justice in Changing Societies* (Christian Lund, ed., London, 1999).

Cambodian Legal Resources Development Centre (Sok Siphana, ed.), *International Conference on Cambodian Legal and Judicial Reform in the Context of Sustainable Development*, (CLRDC, Phnom Penh, 1998).

Centre for Advanced Study, *Cambodia Report: Legal and Political Development in Cambodia*, (Centre for Advanced Study, Phnom Penh, Vol. 3, Issue I, May-June 1997).

Chr. Michelsen Institute, *Evaluation of Danish Support to Promotion of Human*

Rights and Democratisation, (Second Draft, CMI, Bergen, Norway, 18 October 1999).

CIDA, *CIDA's Support for Human Rights and Democratization*, (CIDA, Ottawa, 1998).

CIDA, *Report from the Legal/Judicial Roundtable*, (CIDA, Meech Lake, Canada, 1996).

Clapham, Andrew, "Mainstreaming Human Rights at the United Nations: The Challenge for the First High Commissioner for Human Rights", in *Collected Courses of the Academy of European Law*, (Vol. VII, Book 2, 159-234, Kluwer, Netherlands, 1999).

Comision de Fortalecimiento de la Justicia, *Una Nueva Justicia Para la Paz: Resumen Ejecutivo del Informe Final de la Comision de Fortalecimiento de la Justicia*, (Guatemala, April 1998).

Comision de Modernizacion del Organismo Judicial, *Plan de Modernizacion del Organismo Judicial 1997-2002*, (Guatemala, August 1997).

Commission for Historical Clarification, *Guatemala: Memory of Silence: TZ'INIL NA'TAB'AL, Report of the Commission for Historical Clarification*, Conclusions and Recommendations, (CEH, Guatemala, 1999).

Cooter, Robert, *The Rule of State Law Versus the Rule of Law State: Economic Analysis of the Legal Foundations of Development*, (World Bank, Washington, 1996).

Council of Europe, *Activities for the Development and Consolidation of Democratic Stability (ADACS): Programme 1998*, (Council of Europe Doc. SG/INF/(98)2, 1998).

Curtis, Grant, *Cambodia Reborn?: The Transition to Democracy and Development*, (Brookings Institution and UNRISD, Geneva, 1998).

Danish Centre for Human Rights / Institute of International Education, *The Role of Voluntary Organizations in Emerging Democracies*, (DCHR, Copenhagen, 1993).

Defensoria Maya, *Suk'B'Anik: Administracion de Justicia Maya*, (Defensoria Maya, Guatemala, 1999).

Department of Justice of South Africa, *Justice Vision 2000*, (Government of South Africa, Pretoria, 1997).

European Commission, *Accession Partnership Bulgaria*, (EC, Brussels, Doc. No. DG 1A F/6, n.d.).

European Commission, *Evaluation of the PHARE and TACIS Democracy*

Programme 1992-1997, (EU, Brussels, 1998).

European Commission, *Commission Communication to the Parliament: Democratization, the rule of law, respect for human rights and good governance: the challenges of the partnership between the European Union and the ACP States*, (EU, Brussels, 12 March 1998 (COM(98)146).

European Union, *The European Union's Democracy and Human Rights Initiative for ACP States, Eastern and Central Europe, the New Independent States & Mongolia and for Specific Related Activities (independently from their geographical location): Guidelines for Applicants*, (EU, Brussels, n.d.).

EU & EUHRFSA, *The European Union Foundation for Human Rights in South Africa: Mid-Term Programme Evaluation*, (EU, Brussels and Johannesburg, 1998).

Feeney, Patricia, *Accountable Aid: Local Participation in Major Projects*, (Oxfam, Oxford, 1998).

Foreign and Commonwealth Office (UK Government), *Human Rights: Guidelines for Posts and Departments*, (FCO, London, March 1999).

Fuhrer, Helmut, *The Story of Official Development Assistance: A History of the Development Assistance Committee and the Development Co-operation Directorate in Dates, Names and Figures*, (OECD, Paris, Doc. No. OCDF/GD(94)67, 1996).

Gender Manual Consortium, *Making Women's Rights Real: A Resource Manual on Women, Gender, Human Rights and the Law*, (GMS and the European Union Foundation for Human Rights in South Africa, Pretoria, 1999).

Gorman, Siobhan, *Gender and Development in Cambodia: An Overview*, (Cambodia Development Resource Institute, Working Paper No. 10, Phnom Penh, June 1999),

Hammergren, Linn, *Judicial Training and Justice Reform*, (USAID, Centre for Democracy and Governance, Washington, n.d.).

Hammergren, Linn, *Rule of Law: Approaches to Justice Reform, and What We Have Learned*, (USAID, Washington, April 1998).

Hausermann, Julia, *A Human Rights Approach to Development*, (London, Rights and Humanity, 1998).

IDASA, (D. Budlender, ed.), *The Fourth Women's Budget*, (IDASA, Cape Town, 1999).

Instancia Coordinadora Para La Modernizacion Del Sector Justicia (ICMSJ), *Plan Estrategico Sectorial*, 1998-2002, (ICMSJ, Guatemala, 1998).

Instancia Coordinadora Para La Modernizacion Del Sector Justicia (ICMSJ), *Politica del Estado Contra El Crimen*, (ICMSJ, Guatemala, 1998).

ISA, European Institute of Sussex University, and GJW Europe, *Final Report: Evaluation of the Phare and Tacis Democracy Programme, 1992-1997*, (ISA/EI/GJW, Brighton and Hamburg, 1997).

Junta Directive a Traves de la Unidad Academica del Colegio de Abogados y Notarios de Guatemala, *Diagnóstico de la Administración de la Justicia Penal 1996-1998*, (Guatemala, February 1998).

Kaplan, Alan, *The Development of Capacity*, (NGLS Development Dossier, UN Non-Governmental Liaison Service, Geneva, 1999).

Kingdom of Cambodia, Royal Government, Council of Ministers, *Programme Spécial: Réforme de l'Administration Publique, 1999-2003*, (KOC, Phnom Penh, January 1999).

Kingdom of Cambodia, Royal Government, *Socio-Economic Development Requirements and Proposals*, (KOC, Phnom Penh, January 1999).

Lamontagne, Veronique, *Background Paper on Legal and Judicial Co-operation*, (CIDA, Meech Lake, Canada, April 19, 1996).

Lawyers Committee for Human Rights, *Abandoning the Victims: The UN Advisory Services Programme in Guatemala*, (February 1990, New York).

Lawyers Committee for Human Rights and the Institute for Policy Research and Advocacy, *In the Name of Development: Human Rights and the World Bank in Indonesia*, (New York, LCHR/ELSAM, 1995).

Lawyers Committee for Human Rights and Provea, *Halfway to Reform: The World Bank and the Venezuelan Justice System*, (New York, LCHR/Provea, 1996).

Lund, Christian (ed.), *Development and Rights: Negotiating Justice in Changing Societies,* (Frank Cass, London, 1999).

Maren, Michael, *The Road to Hell: The Ravaging Effects of Foreign Aid and International Charity,* (The Free Press, New York, 1997).

Marotta, Francesca, "The Blue Flame and the Gold Shield, Human Rights Training for Law Enforcement", in *International Peacekeeping*, (Cass, Essex, Vol. 6, No. 4, Winter 1999, at pp 69-92).

Messick, Richard, *Judicial Reform: A Survey of the Issues,* (World Bank, Draft of August 1997).

Mokhiber, Craig, *Rule of Law Development in the West Bank and Gaza Strip: Survey and Status of the Development Effort*, (UNSCO, Gaza, July 1997).

Mokhiber, Craig, "The United Nations Programme of Technical Cooperation in the Field of Human Rights", in *Human Rights Monitoring Procedures: A Textbook on Petitioning and Lobbying International Organizations*, (Raoul Wallenberg Institute of Human Rights and Humanitarian Law, 1997, forthcoming).

Neam, Koy, *Introduction to the Cambodian Judicial Process*, (The Asia Foundation, Phnom Penh, 1998).

Netherlands Institute of Human Rights (SIM), *Human Rights in Development Cooperation*, (SIM Special No. 22, Utrecht, 1998).

Novib, *Human Rights and Development: Novib's Challenges in the Field of Human Rights* (Novib, The Hague, 1997).

Novib, Programma Evaluatie Nr. 75, *Promoting Human Rights and Democratic Processes with Gender Equity: NOVIB in Guatemala*, (Novib, Guatemala, September 1998).

OECD/DAC, *Conflict, Peace and Development Cooperation on the Threshold of the 21st Century*, (DAC Development Cooperation Guideline Series, OECD, Paris 1998).

OECD/DAC, Expert Group on Aid Evaluation, *Evaluation of Programmes Promoting Participatory Development and Good Governance*, (OECD, Paris, 1997).

OECD/DAC, *Final Report of the DAC Working Group on Participatory Development and Good Governance*, (OECD, Paris, 1997).

OECD/DAC, *Participatory Development and Good Governance*, (DAC Development Cooperation Guideline Series, OECD, Paris 1995).

Oxfam, *Investing in People: Oxfam UK/I in Cambodia*, (Oxfam UK/I, Phnom Penh, 1997).

Rishmawi, Mona, "Human Rights in Development: UN Technical Cooperation in the Field of Human Rights", in *40th International Seminar for Diplomats: the Universal Protection of Human Rights: Translating International Commitments into National Action*, (Austrian Federal Ministry for Foreign Affairs, August 1997).

SANGOCO, *Development Update: Does Development Have to be Democratic?* (Development Update, Vol. 2 No. 1, South African National NGO Coalition and Interfund, 1998).

Santos Pais, Marta, *A Human Rights Conceptual Framework for UNICEF*, (UNICEF, Innocenti Essay No. 9, Florence, 1999).

Sen, Amartya, *Development as Freedom*, (Knopf, New York, 1999).

Tisch, S., and Wallace, M., *Dilemmas of Development Assistance: The What,*

Why and Who of Foreign Aid, (Westview Press, Boulder, Colorado, 1994).

Tomasevski, Katarina, *Between Sanctions and Elections: Aid Donors and Their Human Rights Performance,* (Pinter, London, 1997).

Tomasevski, Katarina, *Development Aid and Human Rights,* (St. Martin's Press, New York, 1989).

Toope, Stephen, *Programming in Legal and Judicial Reform: An Analytical Framework for CIDA Engagement*, (CIDA, Montreal, 1997).

Tvedt, Terje, *Angels of Mercy or Development Diplomats?: NGOs and Foreign Aid,* (Africa World Press, Oxford, 1998).

UNITAR, *The United Nations Transitional Authority in Cambodia (UNTAC): Debriefing and Lessons*, (Kluwer Law International, London, 1995).

United Nations, *Advisory Services and Technical Cooperation in the Field of Human Rights*, (UN Centre for Human Rights, Fact Sheet No. 3, rev. 1, Geneva, 1996).

United Nations, *Human Rights: A Compilation of International Instruments*, Vol. I, (First and Second Parts, International Instruments, United Nations, New York and Geneva, 1994, Doc. No. ST/HR/1/Rev.5).

United Nations, *The United Nations and Cambodia*, (United Nations Blue Book series, Vol. II, UN, New York, 1995).

United Nations, *The United Nations and Human Rights: 1945-1995*, (United Nations Blue Book Series, Vol. VII, UN, New York, 1995).

United Nations, Commission on Human Rights, *(Annual) Report(s) of the UN Secretary General on Advisory Services and Technical Cooperation in the Field of Human Rights*, (most recently UN Doc. E/CN.4/1999/99 of 5 February 1999).

United Nations Development Programme, *Human Development and Human Rights: Report of the Oslo Symposium*, (UNDP, OHCHR, and the Royal Ministry of Foreign Affairs of Norway, Oslo, 1998).

United Nations Development Programme, *Human Rights in Bulgaria 1998*, (UNDP, Sophia, 1998).

United Nations Development Programme, *Integrating Human Rights with Sustainable Human Development*, (UNDP, New York, 1998).

United Nations Development Programme, *Survey of UNDP Activities in Human Rights,* (UNDP/MDGD, New York, August 1999).

UNDP/OHCHR Joint Task Force, *Report on the First Year of Cooperation, Implementation of the Memorandum of Understanding of 4 March 1998:*

Implementation Review as at 31 December 1998, (UNDP/OHCHR, 1998, Geneva).

United Nations, Office of the High Commissioner for Human Rights, *Information Note: Technical Cooperation in the Field of Human Rights*, (UNOHCHR, Geneva, December, 1998).

United Nations, Office of the High Commissioner for Human Rights, *System Wide Analysis of United Nations Technical Cooperation Activities in Human Rights Related Areas*, (UN, Geneva, 1999).

Universidad Rafael Landivar, *Acuerdos De Paz*, (URL, Guatemala, 3rd edition, 1998).

USAID, *Democracy and Governance: A Conceptual Framework*, (USAID, Washington, 1998).

USAID, *Self-Study Programme for USAID DG Officers*, (USAID, Washington, n.d.).

USAID, *Weighing in on the Scales of Justice: Strategic Approaches for Donor-Supported Rule of Law Programmes*, (USAID, Washington, February 1994).

Washington Office on Latin America (WOLA), *Demilitarizing Public Order: The International Community, Police Reform and Human Rights in Central America and Haiti*, (WOLA, Washington, November 1995).

Washington Office on Latin America (WOLA), *La Reforma Judicial en Guatemala, 1997-1998: Una Guia Basica Sobre los Problemas, Proocoso y Actores*, (May 1998, Guatemala).

The World Bank, *Assessing Aid: What Works, What Doesn't, and Why*, (IBRD, Oxford University Press, New York, 1998).

The World Bank, *Cambodia Public Expenditure Review, Main Report*, (World Bank, Phnom Penh, January 1999)

The World Bank, *Country Assistance Strategy of the World Bank Group for Bulgaria*, (World Bank, Sophia, April 1998).

The World Bank, *Development and Human Rights: The Role of the World Bank*, (IBRD, Washington, 1998).

The World Bank, *Governance and Development*, (IBRD, Washington, 1992).

The World Bank, *Post-Conflict Reconstruction: The Role of the World Bank*, (IBRD, Washington, 1998).

Web-sites of Aid Providers, NGOs and Institutes Referenced in this Report

International Council on Human Rights Policy: www.ichrp.org

UN Office of the High Commissioner for Human Rights: www.unhchr.ch

United Nations Development Programme: www.undp.org

Development Assistance Committee of the OECD (DAC): www.oecd.org/dac

European Union (EC): www.europa.eu.int

World Bank (IBRD): www.worldbank.org

Soros Foundations Network: www.soros.org

(Soros Constitutional and Legal Policy Institute): www.osi.hu/colpi

Ford Foundation: www.fordfound.org

Amnesty International: www.amnesty.org

International Commission of Jurists: www.icj.org

Human Rights Watch: www.hrw.org

Human Rights Internet: www.hri.ca

Michelsen Institute: www.cmi.no

Australia (AUSAID): www.ausaid.gov.au

Austria: www.bmaa.gv.at

Belgium: www.diplobel.fgov.be

Canada (CIDA): www.acdi-cida.gc.ca

Denmark (DANIDA): www.um.dk

Finland: www.virtual.finland.fi; www.global.finland.fi

France: www.france.diplomatie.fr

Germany (GTZ): www.gtz.de

(BMZ): www.bmz.de

Ireland: www.irlgov.ie

Italy: www.esteri.it

Japan (foreign affairs): www.mofa.go.jp

(JICA): www.jica.go.jp

(JBIC): www.jbic.go.jp

Netherlands: www.bz.minbuza.nl

New Zealand: www.mft.govt.nz

Norway: www.odin.dep.no

Portugal: www.min-nestrangeiros.pt

Spain (AECI): www.aeci.es

Sweden (SIDA): www.sida.se

(Diakonia): www.diakonia.se

(Raada Barnen): www.rb.se

(Forum Syd): www.forumsyd.se

Switzerland (SDC): www.sdc-gov.ch

United Kingdom (DFID): www.dfid.gov.uk

(Foreign & Commonwealth Office): www.hrpd.fco.gov.uk

United States (USAID): www.info.usaid.gov

ABOUT THE INTERNATIONAL COUNCIL ON HUMAN RIGHTS POLICY

The International Council on Human Rights Policy was established in Geneva in 1998, following lengthy international consultation, to conduct practical research into the dilemmas and problems that face organisations working in the field of human rights.

Its Mission Statement reads:

> "The International Council on Human Rights Policy will provide a forum for applied research, reflection and forward thinking on matters of international human rights policy. In a complex world in which interests and priorities compete across the globe, the Council will identify issues that impede efforts to protect and promote human rights and propose approaches and strategies that will advance that purpose.

> The Council will stimulate co-operation and exchange across the non-governmental, governmental and intergovernmental sectors, and strive to mediate between competing perspectives. It will bring together human rights practitioners, scholars and policy-makers, along with those from related disciplines and fields whose knowledge and analysis can inform discussion of human rights policy.

> It will produce research reports and briefing papers with policy recommendations. These will be brought to the attention of policy-makers, within international and regional organisations, in governments and intergovernmental agencies and in voluntary organisations of all kinds.

> In all its efforts, the Council will be global in perspective, inclusive and participatory in agenda-setting and collaborative in method."

The Council starts from the principle that successful policy approaches will accommodate the diversity of human experience. It co-operates with all that share its human rights objectives, including voluntary and private bodies, national governments and international agencies.

Members of the International Council meet annually to set the direction of the Council's Programme. They ensure that the Council's agenda and research draw widely on experience from around the world, and that its programme reflects the diversity of disciplines, regional perspectives, country expertise and specialisations that are essential to maintain the quality of its research.

To implement the programme, the Council employs a small secretariat of six staff, who ensure that projects are well designed and well managed and that research findings are brought to the attention of relevant authorities and those who have a direct interest in the policy areas concerned.

THE INTERNATIONAL COUNCIL

Abdullahi An-Na'im	Professor of Law, Emory University School of Law, Atlanta, United States. Sudan.
Carlos Basombrio*	Director, Instituto de Defensa Legal, Lima. Peru.
Ligia Bolivar	Founder, Legal Defence Program, Venezuelan Program for Human Rights Education and Action (PROVEA). Venezuela.
Theo van Boven	Professor of International Law, University of Maastricht; former Member of the UN Committee on the Elimination of Racial Discrimination. Netherlands.
William Burklé*	Banker; Board Member of Migros. Switzerland.
Antonio Cancade Trindade	Judge, the Inter–American Court of Human Rights; Professor of International Law, University of Brasilia. Brazil.
Stanley Cohen*	Professor of Sociology, London School of Economics. United Kingdom.
Radhika Coomeraswamy	UN Special Rapporteur on Violence against Women; Director, the International Centre for Ethnic Studies, Colombo. Sri Lanka.
Yash Ghai*	Sir Y K Pao Professor of Public Law, Hong Kong.
Thomas Hammarberg*	Ambassador. Sweden.
Bahey El Din Hassan	Director, Cairo Institute for Human Rights Studies. Egypt.
Ayesha Imam*	Co-ordinator, International Solidarity Network of Women Living under Muslim Laws, Region West Africa. Nigeria.
Hina Jilani*	Director, AGHS Legal Aid Cell, Lahore. Pakistan.
Virginia Leary	Distinguished Service Professor of Law, State University of New York at Buffalo. United States of America.
Goenawan Mohamed	Poet; Founder and former Editor of *Tempo* magazine, Indonesia.
Bacre Waly Ndiaye	Lawyer; Director of the Office of the UN High Commissioner for Human Rights in New York. Senegal.
Margo Picken	Associate Fellow at the Centre for International Studies, London School of Economics. United Kingdom.
N. Barney Pityana	Chair, South African Human Rights Commission. South Africa.
Daniel Ravindran	Founder, Asian Forum for Human Rights and Development (Forum-Asia). India.
Dorothy Thomas	Consultant, Shaler Adams Foundation. United States of America.
Renate Weber	Co-President, Romanian Helsinki Committee. Romania.

* **Member of the Executive Board**

ORDER FORM

How to order publications and documents from the Council
If you would like to order copies of this publication or information about other Council publications, please complete this form and return it to the Secretariat at the address given.

This publication

Ref. 104 *Local perspectives: foreign aid to the justice sector – Main Report,*
International Council on Human Rights Policy, 2000,
ISBN 2-940259-04-6, 132pp. 165mm x 220mm.
Available in English. CHF. 36. (+ CHF. 3. – p.&p.).

Qty........... Total:........... (CHF.)

*Local perspectives: foreign aid to the justice sector – Summary of
Findings,* International Council on Human Rights Policy, 2000, 16pp.,
165mm x 220mm. Available in English, French and Spanish.
CHF. 10. – (+ CHF. 3. – p.&p.).

Qty........... Total:........... (CHF.)

Already published

Ref. 112 *The persistence & mutation of racism,* International Council on Human
Rights Policy, 2000, ISBN 2-940259-09-7, 28pp., 165mm x 220mm.
Available in English, French and Spanish.
CHF. 15 . – (+CHF. 3. – p.&p.)

Qty........... Total:........... (CHF.)

Ref. 102 *Performance & legitimacy: national human rights institutions – Main
Report,* International Council on Human Rights Policy, 2000, ISBN 2-
940259-09-0, 110pp. 165mm x 220mm. Available in English.
CHF. 36. – (+ CHF. 3. – p.&p.)

Qty........... Total:........... (CHF.)

*Performance & legitimacy. national human rights institutions –
Summary of Findings.* International Council on Human Rights Policy,
2000, 16pp. 165mm x 220mm. Available in English, French, Spanish &
Bahasa Indonesia.
CHF. 10. – (+ p.&p.)

Qty........... Total:........... (CHF.)

Ref. 103 *Taking Duties Seriously: Individual Duties in International Human Rights
Law – A Commentary,* International Council on Human Rights Policy,
1999, ISBN 2-940259-00-3, 80pp., 165mm x 220mm. Currently available
in English.
CHF. 13.50. – (+ CHF. 3. – p.&p.)

Qty........... Total:........... (CHF.)

Ref. 201 *Hard cases: bringing human rights violators to justice abroad –
A guide to universal jurisdiction,* International Council on Human Rights
Policy, 1999, ISBN 2-940259-01-1, 72pp., 165mm x 220mm. Available in
English. Also available in Spanish from:
IDL
José Toribio Polo 248
Lima 18
Peru
Tel: +511 4 410192; Fax:+511 4 424037
CHF. 15. – (+ Frs. 3. – p.&p.)

Qty........... Total:........... (CHF.)

Forthcoming publications

Ref. 105   *Ends & means: human rights approaches to armed groups*,
International Council on Human Rights Policy, 2000, ISBN 2-940259-02-
X. Publication: July 2000.
CHF. 36. – (+p.&p.)

Qty............ Total:............ (CHF.)

Ref. 107   *Human rights obligations of business under international law*, Draft
report available December 2000.

Method of payment (please complete as appropriate):

Bank transfer: Please transfer to
Account No. S 3218.01.12 Banque Cantonale de Genève, CH–1211 Geneva 2:   ☐

Postal order (Switzerland only) CCP. 17–677255–7:   ☐

Bankers cheque (made payable to International Council on Human Rights Policy): ☐

Credit card: ☐   MasterCard: ☐   Visa: ☐

Card Number: Expiry date:

Name on Card: Signature:

Name:

Organisation:

Address:

Postcode: City: Country:

Telephone: Fax: Email:

Please return the form by mail or fax to:
International Council on Human Rights Policy
48, chemin du Grand-Montfleury
P.O. Box 147,
CH-1290 Versoix, Switzerland
Tel: (41 22) 775 3300
Fax: (41 22) 775 3303